Clodagh's Suppers

Clodagh's Suppers

SUPPERS TO CELEBRATE THE SEASONS

Clodagh McKenna

Photography by Dora Kazmierak

Kyle Books

This book is dedicated to my true love,
Harry Herbert.

An Hachette UK Company
www.hachette.co.uk

First published in Great Britain in 2018 by
Kyle Books, an imprint of Kyle Cathie Ltd
Carmelite House
50 Victoria Embankment
London EC4Y 0DZ
www.kylebooks.co.uk

ISBN: 978 0 857834 966

Publisher: Joanna Copestick
Editor: Vicky Orchard
Design: Lucy Gowans
Creative director: Clodagh McKenna
Photography: Dora Kazmierak
Food styling: Lizzie Harris
Props styling: Wei Tang
Production: Nic Jones, Gemma John and Katherine Hockley

A Cataloguing in Publication record for this title is available
from the British Library

Printed and bound in China

10 9 8 7 6 5 4 3 2 1

Contents

Introduction

I am never happier than seeing my loved ones sitting around the table with smiles on their faces as they enjoy delicious home-cooked food in a beautiful setting. The importance of supper at home has been instilled in me since I was a child. I have so many amazing memories of suppers shared with my family when we were children. The table laid with proper linen, fresh flowers and bowls of home-cooked food. The suppers nearly always ended with someone singing a song or one of us giving some sort of performance. This has now become a tradition at my suppers in my own home, sometimes even beginning before the main course hits the table! For me, this is what life is all about, enjoying memorable moments together. I truly hope that by sharing all my recipes, tips, tablescape ideas, menus and cocktails that you will start hosting your own suppers at home too.

I call it a supper rather than a dinner and you may wonder what the difference is. For me a supper is relaxed and informal – a delicious loaf of my Rosemary Clodagh Bread (page 203) on a wooden board in the centre of the table with hands diving in to tear chunks off to dip in a seasonal soup, such as my Smoked Haddock & Corn Chowder (page 108). A supper is all about sharing food made by you around a table where your friends and family feel completely at home and relaxed.

I have created menus with a starter, main and dessert to give you an idea of what flavours work well together and that is also balanced. I have planned them so that the courses aren't too laborious and some you can even cook a day ahead to make your supper stress free. You can also swap out the recipes to create the menu that you love best, but I would suggest trying to keep within the seasons as the food will always taste and look better.

To kick off my suppers, I love to set up a cocktail table with one seasonal special, such as my Sparkling Rhubarb Cocktail (page 182) in the spring or the Blackberry & Rosemary Cocktail (page 186) in the autumn. I also serve a delicious seasonal nibble, such as the Spring Pea Guacamole with Radishes (page 191), on the table with the cocktails. Always a fun way to start the evening! In the summer I will have this set up on a table with fresh flowers in the garden and during the colder months I'll create the cocktail area in a more cosy setting by the fire.

Every week I develop recipes in my kitchen for my weekly *Evening Standard* column and for television shows, such as Channel 4's *Sunday Brunch*, the NBC *Today* show and *The Marilyn Denis Show* in Canada, as well as many others including my weekly Youtube series. So there are lots of recipes to test every week and my favourites always end up at my suppers at home, where my best and worst critics give their reviews! I am so excited to share the 120 recipes that came out on top in the pages ahead. All the recipes have suggested curated supper menus but of course there are many ideas for soups, salads, pâtés, one-pot suppers, cakes and so on that are perfect for everyday cooking.

I have laid out the book to make it as simple as possible for you to find all that you need for creating the perfect supper at home! The first section is about the preparation, including a checklist of what you need to prepare before everyone arrives. This is followed by some beautiful seasonal tablescapes to give you lots of inspiraton and ideas on how to easily turn your table into a visually spectacular setting. The second section focuses on the menu and recipes, to help you create a well-balanced menu that suits each season and occasion. I have also included festive occasions such as Easter, Christmas and Thanksgiving. Lastly a chapter on cocktails and nibbles to serve for when your guests arrive as well as some delicious treats for after supper like my Rosewater & Pistachio Florentines (page 194) that just take 15 minutes to make.

Creating a magical supper is so much fun and will fill your home with special memories. Plan it out so that it's not a stressful task but an enjoyable one where you can unleash your creative side. Sprigs of branches, herbs or flowers along the table with ambient candles dotted throughout, dried lavendar on everyone's napkins or figs with place settings popped in a slit of the fruit, are all so easy to create. One delicious pot of homemade food is so much more special than three courses of shop-bought ready meals. Keep it simple and cook the dishes that you love the most. Candles lit, playlist on, table laid, food cooked - all that's left is to make yourself one of my delicious cocktails and let it be a night to remember.

Happy Suppers!

Love Clo xx

The Menu

The menu is undoubtedly the most important part of my supper party and I always carve out a bit of time to create a well-balanced menu with courses complementing each other. I love getting into bed early with pen and paper a few nights before I host a supper and leisurely writing a menu that I will get excited about cooking.

IN SEASON

The first thing that I do is write out a list of foods that are in season. This is so important to me as seasonal ingredients always taste so much better and I love being present with the passing of the seasons. It creates such a memorable occasion – indeed all the recipes in the pages ahead mark the seasons. Seeing the first of the rhubarb in my local vegetable shop and making it into a syrup for a sparkling rhubarb cocktail – that first delicious sip has me right back to when I was a child and my mother would make butter pastry rhubarb tarts. That is exactly what suppers are all about for me – creating memories that will live on and on... Cooking with the seasons allows me to get excited about the coming months and the produce they will bring.

BALANCING THE MENU

When I am planning my supper, I start with the dish that I am most excited about cooking and then I build around it. Here's what I always stick to. If I am cooking fish or something spicy for the main course, then I will tend to serve a light, refreshing dessert to cleanse the palate. To start the supper, a vegetable- or fish-based dish works very well, like my Gazpacho with Cucumber & Dill Salsa (page 71) or Crab, Blood Orange & Fennel Salad (page 154). When it comes to a meat-based main course, I serve soups or other light meat dishes as a starter. I am never in favour of spicy or creamy courses following one another – I wouldn't serve a cream-based dish after a chowder as it would be too rich. The trick is for your guests' palates to be refreshed with different flavours after each course. The menu also goes with the season – I tend to eat more hearty foods in the winter (I think we all do!) and so during the colder months you can get away with serving more filling courses throughout the supper. In the summer, we look for lighter, fresher-tasting foods, as we don't crave the warming comfort dishes of the colder months.

The Prep

Once you have decided on your menu, the next thing to start thinking about is how best to prepare and get organised. Everyone knows how to write a shopping list, but it might also help to have a checklist of everything you need to do beforehand, from choosing the wine to creating a playlist and even to thinking about who's going to sit where. This is my helpful guide to everything that you need to consider before your supper.

SHOPPING LISTS

I am a bit of a list queen, it has been said... I like to be organised and making lists is how I take the stress out of any tasks. When it comes to hosting a supper at home, the shopping can be the most mundane part of it. I separate my shopping list into two sections. Dry ingredients and fresh ingredients. I go through my cupboards and check my stock of dry foods, candles, fizzy water, wine, etc and then make my list and do the order online and have them delivered days before, which saves time and energy. The fresh ingredients I spend more time on; if it's fish that I am cooking, I take the time to go to a good fishmonger, as the better the quality, the better your cooking will taste! For meat, it is always worth the trip to a good butcher. If you are on a budget, then you'll have a better range of cheaper, less-used cuts from the butcher, which is also a great place to get bones for broths and stocks if you are making a soup or risotto. The fresh ingredients I shop for the day before.

TABLETOP WARE

Don't leave this until the last minute, or your guests could be eating off paper plates! Count how many guests you have for supper, then pull out all your crockery, cutlery and glassware. Decide which dish you are going to use for each course and count how many you have to ensure there's enough for everyone. Do the same with your glassware, matching them to the wines and water you are serving. And then the platters (if using) for serving the food.

HERE'S MY FOOLPROOF SUPPER CHECKLIST

• Count cutlery, crockery and glassware

• Polish silverware and glassware

• Cocktail set up – ice, shaker, liquor, soda water, lemons, cocktail glasses and tray

• Linen – napkins and tablecloth

• Two good playlists – one for before and during supper and one for afters (if your suppers are like mine and you like a post-supper boogie!)

• Candlesticks and holders, cleaned and polished

• Candles for the table, around the house and a nice smelling candle in the bathroom

• Vases for flowers cleaned and ready for arranging

• Flowers for the table, around the house and also a small arrangement beside the sink in the bathroom

• Water jugs filled with ice, mint and lemon slices

• Butter sliced on small butter dishes with a little sprig of fresh rosemary

• Small bowls for sea salt

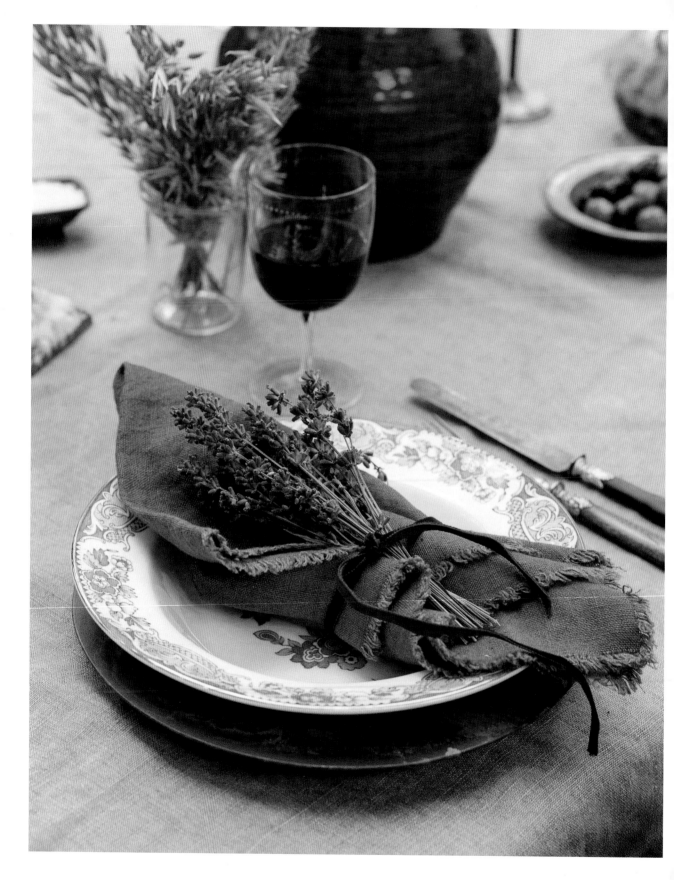

The Table

Along with creating the menu, styling the table is definitely one of my favourite parts of planning a supper. I love being able to transform my table into a space that reflects the seasons and the ingredients that I'm going to use. In this section, I share with you the best ways to create a beautifully set table that will make any supper even more special, and the great thing is that it can be done in advance leaving you more time to enjoy cooking.

HANDWRITTEN MENUS

A handwritten menu perched in the middle of your supper table sets such a lovely personal tone. This can be done really simply by using nice postcards or A5 blank white cards. I always write them in pencil (easy to rub out mistakes) and draw little illustrations of vegetables or festive images along the side. The following day, I clip the menu on my menu string in my kitchen as I love to stop and read back through them.

LINEN

Texture is important to create a beautiful table, and good linen will soften and warm hard textures, such as wood or glass. It is worth investing in a good tablecloth and napkins that will last you through the years. I love natural linen as the more you use and wash it the better it becomes. I have four different sets of linen – one for each of the four seasons. Soft blush pink for summer, mustard for autumn, teal green for winter and soft sage green for spring. The linen for me is the canvas to the table, and I build upon that, introducing colours through flowers, and crockery that will reflect the season and work with the linen. Linen napkins bring a softness to the table that you won't get from using paper. As well as linen, I have a drawer where I keep all different colours and textures of ribbon – these are to tie napkins with sprigs of seasonal flowers or herbs.

CROCKERY, CUTLERY AND GLASSWARE

Most of my crockery, cutlery and glassware come from second-hand stores and markets. This is the best place to pick up special pieces for your table without it costing a fortune. Don't worry about not getting matching sets – I love to mix and match as it brings more personality to the table. Also keep an eye out for flower vases, jugs and small bowls that can be used for sea salt, sauces and butter.

I recently picked up a whole set of Irish china for €20 in a charity shop in County Kerry, Ireland and these mixed charity-shop-bought plates look so pretty even though they don't match. It's well worth taking an afternoon out to forage through a second-hand store to find treasures for your table.

FLOWERS

Like my food, I always use seasonal flowers. Seeing the seasons visually throughout my home makes me so happy and on my table it creates a seasonal moment. The flowers are fresher, more pert and usually cheaper when you buy in season. If you live in the country or you visit the country a lot, go and pick wild flowers from the hedgerows. I do this most weekends. I like to use one to three types of flowers on a table, as any more in the mix and it gets too busy. A lot of the time I just use one variety, even if it's just a simple bluebell in spring, as it makes such an impact.

When I'm using just one type of flower, I use lots of them and place one to two stems in different-sized jars or vases around the table. I also place one on everyone's napkin as part of the place setting. Ivy running down the centre of a rectangular table can look great; add little night lights throughout and small jars of flowers. Big sprigs of tree branches look fantastic at the end of the table or on a side board – you can do this at any time of the year. The idea is to bring as much seasonality to the supper table as possible.

The Table SPRING

For me, a spring table is all about adding freshness and vitality to the table. Beautiful shades of green with fresh white flowers and green stems are a staple during spring. Lots of stem vases with two or three wild garlic flowers or snowdrops look so pretty running down the centre of the table, with a large vase in the centre or to the side filled with large branches with buds about to open. Bluebells are such a pretty spring flower and look lovely in stem glasses or as a sprig on every napkin. A flood of daffodils can look really cheerful on a white linen tablecoth or try them as small bunches tied with twine on each napkin.

I also love decorating the table with seasonal vegetables. At this time of year, fresh radishes with their long, green leaves look fabulous dotted along the table, or again placed on each napkin. Green linen napkins, sage or olive, are my favourite shades during spring. They look beautiful on a wooden table or on a fresh white or cream linen tablecloth. Matched with pewter plates or pottery it all looks stunning. A spring table with delicate simple flowers and soft green seasonal colours really captures this special time of year and brightens up your home after a long winter.

The Table SUMMER

This summer table that I have created is dressed with a soft, blush pink, washed linen cloth. I then use blue and white Danish or Portuguese-style crockery with soft, blush pink, washed linen napkins folded on top and wrapped with pink velvet ribbon. I then insert the cutlery under the ribbon. Along the table I have single stems of peonies or tulips, which look so delicate and pretty.

I love picking wild flowers at this time of year and creating a meadow-like feel for the table. Little bundles of cottage roses in between tealights in pretty glass jars or brass stem candlesticks are so romantic.

When it comes to the end of the summer and heritage tomatoes are available at farmers' markets, I also love to use those for decorating the table. The different colours and varieties of tomatoes look so beautiful. Soft, blue linen is also gorgeous in the summer and if you are near the coast do go and collect some pretty shells to place on pale blue napkins. Larger flat shells can also be used as butter, salt and salsa dishes.

The Table AUTUMN

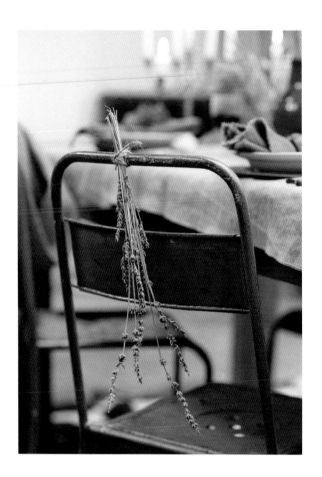

Autumn is my favourite table to create. The interesting different shades of brown, mustard and purple all look so stunning on the table. I love a mustard-coloured linen tablecloth set off with lilac linen napkins and small bunches of dried lavender sprigs tied together with twine. It reminds me of harvest-time in Provence. Big bunches of wheatsheaves in vases at each end of the table or the centre, and other dried flowers in small vases across the table also look beautiful. I tie small bunches of dried lavender on the backs of the chairs which not only looks pretty but also smells amazing.

Another great look is blackberry or sloe berry sprigs on each napkin with longer sprigs in vases along the table. There are also so many amazing varieties of small ornamental squashes that you can buy in your local vegetable store or market available in wonderful colours that look fantastic.

Another idea is brown leaves that you can press between books to make sure they don't curl up and then place them on each table setting with acorns on top. They also make great name places as you can write on them! Large fig leaves used as charger plates or in the centre of the table under bowls or candles look fabulous, too.

The Table WINTER

Fresh figs, heather, pussy willow, red berry branches, pomegranates and clementines are all in season during the winter months and make any table look so magical. In this setting I am using my teal blue linen tablecloth and napkins, which not only give a lovely warmth but also go so well with winter reds and the earthy colours of fresh figs and heather. I buy the heather in pots which I keep in the garden, then I cut the sprigs when I need them to decorate my table. Simple bundles of heather tied together on a napkin look so lovely. I also use fresh figs as table settings and by making a slit halfway down (cutting from the top) you can pop name cards into them. Big, beautiful sprigs of pussy willow look fabulous as a centrepiece to a winter table, with a few sprigs of red berry branches dotted throughout. Add a few fairy lights (battery powered) around them for an instant festive ambience!

When I am planning my festive tables during the winter, I often use clementines to decorate the place settings. Try to find the ones with the green leaves on them so you can write your guests' names on the leaf. Arrange halved pomegranates along the table as the jewels inside the fruit look so prettty and festive. Finally don't forget to add lots of candles to light up your Christmas table!

Ambience

LIGHTING

This is the most vital element besides the food for a supper. A brightly lit room
is my idea of a total nightmare as it makes me feel tired incredibly quickly and
there is nothing relaxing about bright lights! It takes no time to quickly check
the bulbs on your lamps and there are many lovely soft light bulbs available. Next
up, overhead lights never work for me so just turn them off. Having had my own
restaurants for many years I firmly believe that most people don't like these either.

What I have learned is that you simply can't have too many candles! To be really
picky the flicker of a candle should be lower than your chin and not at eye-level
or above as this creates the most flattering and soft light. This might sound a
bit over the top but it's always good to know when you are buying candlesticks. I
adore brass candlesticks, which can be found on eBay or at second-hand stores.
Also, have fun with coloured candles – my favourites are natural wax but I also
love olive green and blush pink which can really add to the look of the table. Don't
forget about the area surrounding your table, such as mantelpieces, side tables
and drinks cabinets. Floods of tealights in brown paper bags or glass jars at the
entrance or around the garden can look gorgeous but remember to put out quite a
few either dotted in a line or bundled together to make an impact.

COMFORT

The seating is so important for your guests to enjoy a comfortable evening. If your
dining or garden chairs are hard, then the easiest thing to do is put cushions on
them. I like all my cushion covers to match and for the colour to be neutral so that
it will go well with all my different tablecloths. My cushions are white with navy
pinstripes and I have 20 of them just in case for larger suppers. The next thing
is warmth. When I am having a supper in the garden, I drape wraps, pashminas
or small blankets over the backs of chairs. It's lovely for your guests not to worry
about getting chilly and it keeps the party going on longer! Plus it looks lovely.

MUSIC

If you follow me on social media, or have been to my house for supper, then you
will know already how much I love music and a good boogie or sing-song after
supper! I like to have three playlists for a supper. One for cocktails on arrival,
something jazzy or Motown (Nina Simone is a favourite or nothing beats the
Buena Vista Social Club), then for supper something more folky, such as Hozier.
For after supper, the playlist should be either for a sing-song or a fun dance – Tina
Turner is always on my list. So take some time out to create your playlist a week
before you host your supper, it's fun and it adds such a wonderful ambience.

Spring Suppers

Menus

SPRING SUPPER FOR TWO

SOFT-BOILED EGG WITH CRUMBLED
BLACK PUDDING & ASPARAGUS

LOBSTER LINGUINE

MY ITALIAN BAKED RICOTTA CHEESECAKE

SPRING ROAST LAMB SUPPER

WATERCRESS SOUP WITH ROSEMARY
& TOASTED PINE NUTS

ROAST BUTTERFLIED LAMB
WITH SALSA VERDE

LEMON MERINGUE PIE

WILD GARLIC FOREST SUPPER

WILD GARLIC SOUP WITH TOASTED
ALMONDS & SHEEP'S CHEESE

WILD GARLIC TAGLIATELLE WITH
GOAT'S CHEESE, COURGETTES
& TOASTED ALMONDS

COCONUT & LEMON CLOUD CAKE

ST PATRICK'S DAY SUPPER

SALT-BAKED POTATO WITH CRÈME
FRAÎCHE & IRISH TROUT CAVIAR

SODA-BREADED BACON CHOPS WITH
IRISH HONEY & WHISKEY DIP
& COLCANNON

GUINNESS CARAMEL TIRAMISU

EASTER SUPPER

SPRING PEA, PEA SHOOT, PANCETTA &
GOAT'S CHEESE SALAD

HAZELNUT & HERB-CRUSTED
LAMB CUTLETS WITH PEA & WILD
GARLIC PURÉE

RHUBARB, ROSEWATER & PISTACHIO
GALETTES

FISH SUPPER

DUBLIN BAY PRAWN CEVICHE

SEA BREAM & CLAMS WITH PURPLE
SPROUTING BROCCOLI, ROMESCO
& CRUNCHY SEEDS

LEMON VERBENA POSSETS

SPRING GATHERING

ASPARAGUS MIMOSA

WATERCRESS BUTTERED CHICKEN WITH
BROAD BEANS & ROSEMARY POTATOES

RHUBARB & CRYSTALLISED GINGER
UPSIDE-DOWN CAKE

Wild Garlic Soup with Toasted Almonds & Sheep's Cheese

SERVES 6

This wild garlic soup is so deliciously pungent, just one spoonful transports me back to the forest floor of wild garlic where I picked it. I have added a topping of toasted almonds and sheep's cheese for texture and a contrast of flavour. You could use hazelnuts, Brazil nuts or pine nuts instead of the almonds, and during other seasons, you can replace the wild garlic with spinach, watercress or wild nettle tops.

50g butter

300g potatoes, peeled and roughly chopped

100g onions, roughly chopped

1 litre hot chicken or vegetable stock

200g wild garlic leaves, thoroughly washed and chopped

100ml double cream

sea salt and freshly ground black pepper

FOR THE TOPPING

50g blanched almonds, toasted and chopped

80g sheep's cheese, such as feta, crumbled

80ml extra virgin olive oil

wild garlic flowers, thoroughly washed, to garnish

Place a heavy-based saucepan over a medium heat and add the butter. Once the butter has melted, add the potatoes and onions, stir well and cover the pan with a lid. Reduce the heat to low and leave the vegetables to sweat for about 10 minutes, stirring occasionally.

Add the hot stock and wild garlic leaves and bring to the boil. Then reduce the heat and simmer, uncovered, for about 10 minutes until the potatoes are tender.

Transfer the soup to a blender or food-processor, or use a hand blender, and blend to a smooth consistency.

Return the soup to the saucepan (if necessary) and season with salt and pepper. Stir in the cream and place over a medium heat for just 2 minutes to warm through.

Meanwhile, for the topping, mix the almonds, sheep's cheese and extra virgin olive oil together in a small bowl.

Pour the soup into warmed bowls, spoon the almond and sheep's cheese mixture on top of each serving and sprinkle with wild garlic flowers to garnish.

Asparagus Mimosa

SERVES 4

These green spears look so beautiful on the table. And the combination of the roasted asparagus with the fluffy sieved (or finely chopped) hard-boiled egg flecked on top, finished with the sweet and citrusy flavours of the lemon and basil in the dressing, is so delicious! You can serve this up on one or two big platters if you are feeding a large crowd, and the eggs and dressing can be prepared the day before, so it's quite an easy starter to pull together. I've also made this just as successfully using stemmed purple sprouting broccoli in place of the asparagus.

20 asparagus spears, woody ends trimmed

1 tablespoon olive oil

2 hard-boiled eggs

sea salt and freshly ground black pepper

FOR THE DRESSING

juice of 1 lemon

1 tablespoon finely chopped shallot

1 tablespoon torn basil leaves

1 teaspoon Dijon mustard

⅛ teaspoon freshly ground black pepper

80ml extra virgin olive oil

Preheat the oven to 180°C/gas mark 4.

Toss the asparagus spears in the olive oil and season with salt and pepper. Place on a baking tray and bake for 10 minutes, or roast on a hot griddle pan over a high heat for 5 minutes, turning often so that they are evenly cooked.

For the dressing, whisk the lemon juice, shallot, basil and mustard together in a small bowl, and season with salt and the pepper. Then add the extra virgin olive oil in a slow stream, whisking constantly.

Shell and halve the eggs, then push through a medium-mesh sieve into another small bowl or finely chop.

Toss the baked or roasted asparagus with 1 tablespoon of the dressing in a large bowl, then divide the dressed asparagus between four plates. Spoon the remaining dressing over the asparagus and sprinkle the sieved or chopped egg on top.

Watercress Soup with Rosemary & Toasted Pine Nuts

SERVES 4

There is something so decadent about watercress soup. The first time I made it was when I was a chef many years ago at Ballymaloe House in County Cork, Ireland. You can forage for watercress in the countryside, where it grows on riverside banks. I always soak it in a basin of water with lemon juice added after picking to ensure it's thoroughly clean. The toasted pine nuts add a delicious sweet and nutty flavour, but leave them out if you want a pure watercress soup.

50g butter

350g potatoes, peeled and diced

1 onion, diced

800ml hot chicken or vegetable stock

150g watercress, plus 12 sprigs to garnish, thoroughly washed (see introduction)

½ teaspoon freshly grated nutmeg

100ml crème fraîche

sea salt and freshly ground black pepper

FOR THE TOPPING

50g pine nuts, toasted

1 tablespoon finely chopped rosemary leaves

1 tablespoon crème fraîche

Place a heavy-based saucepan over a medium heat and add the butter. Once the butter has melted, add the potatoes and onion, stir well and cover the pan with a lid. Reduce the heat to low and leave the vegetables to sweat for about 10 minutes, stirring occasionally.

Pour in the hot stock, increase the heat to high and cook, uncovered, for about 10 minutes until the potatoes and onion are completely soft.

Stir in the watercress and nutmeg and cook for a further 5 minutes until the watercress has wilted.

Transfer the soup to a blender or food-processor, or use a hand blender, and blend to a smooth consistency.

Return the soup to the saucepan (if necessary) and season with salt and pepper. Stir in the crème fraîche and place over a medium heat for just 2 minutes to warm through.

Meanwhile, for the topping, mix the pine nuts, rosemary and crème fraîche together in a small bowl.

Serve the soup in warmed bowls, topped with a little of the pine nut mixture and the watercress sprigs to garnish.

Dublin Bay Prawn Ceviche

SERVES 4

I made this starter for a supper I was hosting at chef Mark Hix's Kitchen Library in East London. The supper was a tastescape around Ireland, and this was my Dublin dish. Dublin Bay prawns (langoustines) are plump and juicy, so they work really well as a ceviche, but you can also use fish, such as fresh tuna, sea bass, fluke (flounder) and so on. Don't leave the seafood to marinate for longer than an hour, otherwise it will lose its fresh rawness. Keep the prawn shells for making a bisque – roast them off first and then blend them in a power blender with stock and herbs.

16 raw Dublin Bay prawns (langoustines)

juice of 2 lemons

2 tablespoons olive oil

1 small bunch of wild garlic leaves, thoroughly washed and finely chopped

2 spring onions, very finely sliced

1 teaspoon dried chilli flakes

sea salt

wild garlic flowers, thoroughly washed, to garnish

Remove the heads and shells from the Dublin Bay prawns. Cut into the flesh of each prawn down the back and pull out and discard the black vein that lies just below the surface. This is actually the prawn's digestive tract and needs removing. Rinse the prawns briefly in cold water.

Thinly slice the prawns lengthways, gently pressing your fingers onto the prawns while you cut – this will make it easier to cut thin slices. Divide the thinly sliced prawns between four plates and spread them out so that they cover the whole plate.

For the dressing, whisk the lemon juice, olive oil, wild garlic leaves, spring onions, chilli flakes and a good seasoning of salt together in a small bowl. Pour the dressing over the prawns. Cover and leave in the fridge for an hour.

Serve straight from the fridge, sprinkled with wild garlic flowers to garnish.

Spring Pea, Pea Shoot, Pancetta & Goat's Cheese Salad

SERVES 4

This has to be the prettiest spring salad! The delicate peppery taste of the pea shoots alongside the crispy smoky pancetta, sweet peas and creamy goat's cheese is divine – or try using watercress instead. The dressing lightly scented with orange is my favourite with this salad, but if you are fonder of a lemon dressing, then simply replace the orange with a lemon. I recommend doubling up the dressing recipe, as it will last for up to two weeks in the fridge.

1 tablespoon olive oil

120g diced pancetta

200g pea shoots

200g freshly podded peas

200g soft goat's cheese, crumbled

FOR THE DRESSING

100ml extra virgin olive oil

grated zest and juice of 1 orange

1 teaspoon Dijon mustard

sea salt and freshly ground black pepper

Place a frying pan over a medium–high heat and add the olive oil, followed by the pancetta. Cook the pancetta for about 8 minutes until crispy.

Meanwhile, add all the ingredients for the dressing to a bowl and whisk together well. Season with salt and pepper.

Combine all the remaining ingredients for the salad in a large bowl. Pour over the dressing, add the crispy pancetta and gently toss together.

Divide the salad between four plates and serve.

Salt-baked Potato with Crème Fraîche & Irish Trout Caviar

SERVES 4

One of my all-time favourite dishes to make, this combination of fluffy hot potato filling with silky crème fraîche and peppery flat-leaf parsley, topped with jewels of trout caviar and held within a crispy potato skin, is utterly delicious! I first came up with this recipe when I was curating an Irish menu for Fortnum & Mason in London, and for me it sings of Ireland and it's oh so beautiful... I often make it for a cosy fireside supper on a Friday with a delicious glass of white Burgundy – utter heaven.

4 small baking potatoes, unpeeled and washed

2 tablespoons chopped flat-leaf parsley

200ml crème fraîche

1 tablespoon rapeseed oil

40g trout caviar

sea salt and freshly ground black pepper

Preheat the oven to 200°C/gas mark 6.

Place the potatoes on a baking tray and bake for 40 minutes.

Remove the baked potatoes from the oven and leave until cool enough to handle, then cut them in half lengthways and scoop out the potato flesh into a bowl, leaving the skins intact.

Season the potato flesh with salt and pepper, mash with a fork and then mix in the parsley and 120ml of the crème fraîche. Spoon the potato mixture back into the potato skins, place on the baking tray and brush the skins with the rapeseed oil so that they crisp.

Bake for 15 minutes until the filling is heated through and the skins are crispy.

Remove the filled potato skins from the oven and spoon the remaining crème fraîche on top, followed by a spoonful of the trout caviar. Serve.

Soft-boiled Egg with Crumbled Black Pudding & Asparagus

SERVES 2

These are so simple and fast to make. If it's a cold evening in spring, there is nothing better than to cuddle up for supper in front of the fire and devour these delicious gooey eggs using the asparagus spears to dip into the yolks like toastie soldiers. The black pudding adds a lovely crumbly texture and spicy flavour, but you can leave it out if you're not a fan and add shavings of Parmesan cheese or crumbles of soft goat's cheese instead.

2 organic or free-range eggs

1 tablespoon olive oil

6 asparagus spears, woody ends trimmed

40g black pudding

sea salt and freshly ground black pepper

For runny yolks, cook the eggs in a saucepan of boiling water over a high heat for $5\frac{1}{2}$ minutes.

While the eggs are cooking, set a griddle pan over a medium–high heat and add the olive oil. Place the asparagus spears on the griddle pan and season with salt and pepper, then place the black pudding alongside. Cook both for 5 minutes, turning the spears often so that they are evenly cooked and the black pudding once to cook on both sides.

Once the egg-cooking time is up, immediately transfer the eggs to egg cups. Lightly tap the eggs and remove the tops. Season with salt and pepper, then crumble the black pudding on top of the eggs. Place the egg cups on a plate and arrange the grilled asparagus spears alongside for dipping into the runny yolks.

Watercress Buttered Chicken with Broad Beans & Rosemary Potatoes

SERVES 4

4 chicken supremes (skin-on chicken breasts with the wing bone attached)

sea salt and freshly ground black pepper

FOR THE WATERCRESS BUTTER

80g watercress, chopped, plus extra sprigs to garnish

100g butter, softened

FOR THE ROSEMARY POTATOES

1kg potatoes, sliced

2 tablespoons chopped rosemary leaves

2 garlic cloves, crushed

2 tablespoons olive oil

FOR THE BROAD BEANS

400g fresh broad beans, podded

1 tablespoon olive oil

grated zest and juice of 1 lemon

2 tablespoons chopped mint

Watercress has such a lovely peppery but delicate flavour, so it's delicious with chicken and alongside minted broad beans. I also use this recipe for roasting a whole chicken when I want a more relaxed supper, and I place the broad beans and potatoes in warmed serving bowls and let everyone help themselves. When I am making the watercress butter, I make a big batch, then roll it into a long sausage shape, wrap it in clingfilm and freeze it for slicing and topping other dishes like grilled fish or steamed floury potatoes.

Preheat the oven to 200°C/gas mark 6.

To make the watercress butter, add the chopped watercress and the butter to a bowl and season with salt and pepper, then mix together well – I find using the back of a spoon is the best way to blend the ingredients together.

Smear the watercress butter all over the chicken supremes, working it under the skin of the chicken, too. Place a griddle pan or frying pan over a medium–high heat, add the chicken supremes and brown on each side. Transfer to a roasting tray and roast for 25 minutes.

While the chicken is roasting, parboil the sliced potatoes in a saucepan half-filled with water over a high heat for 10 minutes, then drain and tip into a bowl. Add the rosemary, garlic and olive oil, season with salt and pepper and toss well. Place a frying pan over a medium heat, add the potatoes and fry, tossing every couple of minutes, for about 10 minutes until they are cooked through and a lovely golden colour.

Finally, cook the broad beans. Bring a saucepan of water to the boil over a high heat. Season the water with salt, stir in the broad beans and cook for just 1 minute or until they float to the surface of the water. Drain and toss with the olive oil, lemon zest and juice and mint.

Serve the chicken supremes on warmed plates along with the rosemary potatoes and broad beans, garnished with extra watercress sprigs.

Roast Butterflied Lamb with Salsa Verde

SERVES 8

Butterflied and boned is the fastest and easiest way to roast a joint of lamb, and if you aren't great at carving a joint, you will really love the fact that this roast requires slicing rather than carving. If you would prefer a classic mint sauce to the salsa verde, it's also so simple to make. Whisk together 25g chopped mint, 1 teaspoon of caster sugar, 1 tablespoon of hot water and 2 tablespoons of white wine vinegar and leave to stand for 20 minutes for the flavours to infuse.

3 tablespoons olive oil

2 tablespoons red wine vinegar

3 garlic cloves, finely sliced

2 tablespoons finely chopped rosemary leaves

1.5kg boned and butterflied leg of lamb

sea salt and freshly ground black pepper

FOR THE SALSA VERDE

1 tablespoon white wine vinegar

4 basil sprigs, chopped

2 flat-leaf parsley sprigs, chopped

2 garlic cloves, crushed

2 anchovy fillets, chopped

2 tablespoons capers

200ml extra virgin olive oil

Preheat the oven to 220°C/gas mark 7.

For the marinade, add the olive oil, red wine vinegar, garlic and rosemary to a small bowl, season with salt and pepper and mix together well.

Place the lamb, skin-side up, in a roasting tin and pour over the marinade. Using clean hands, rub the marinade into the lamb and then leave it to sit for 30 minutes. This allows the flavours to be absorbed into the lamb and also gives the meat time to come to room temperature before roasting.

When the 30 minutes is up, roast the marinated lamb for 40 minutes.

While the lamb is roasting, add all the ingredients for the salsa verde to a bowl and mix together well.

Remove the roasted lamb from the oven, cover with a loose tent of foil and leave to rest for 15 minutes.

Thinly slice the roasted lamb onto a warmed platter and spoon the salsa verde down the centre of the lamb. Serve.

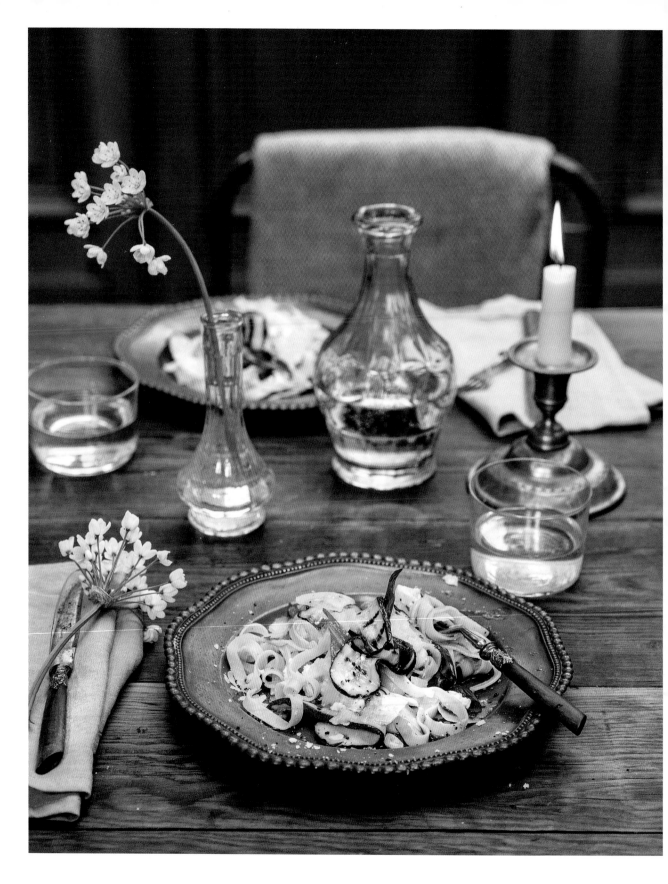

Wild Garlic Tagliatelle with Goat's Cheese, Courgettes & Toasted Almonds

SERVES 4

I love making this dish during the spring because it's so light and fragrant. During the remainder of the year, I simply replace the wild garlic with other fresh herbs that are in season, such as basil, mint or oregano. I sometimes add grilled Dublin Bay prawns (langoustines), prawns or chicken to this dish for a weekday one-course supper.

2 tablespoons olive oil

4 courgettes, cut into ribbons using a vegetable peeler

500g fresh tagliatelle

4 tablespoons chopped wild garlic leaves

200g soft goat's cheese

100g blanched almonds, toasted and chopped

50g Parmesan cheese, shaved

sea salt and freshly ground black pepper

Place a griddle pan or frying pan over a medium–high heat and add 1 tablespoon of the olive oil. Add the courgette ribbons to the pan and cook for 2 minutes on each side. Season with salt and pepper.

Meanwhile, bring a large saucepan of salted water to the boil over a high heat. Stir in the fresh pasta and cook for 3 minutes. Drain the cooked pasta and return to the pan, then add the remaining tablespoon of olive oil and gently toss to coat.

Stir the wild garlic, grilled courgette ribbons, soft goat's cheese and almonds into the pasta, and season with salt and pepper.

Serve the tagliatelle on a warmed platter or individual plates, with the Parmesan shavings sprinkled on top.

Sea Bream & Clams with Purple Sprouting Broccoli, Romesco & Crunchy Seeds

SERVES 4

4 sea bream fillets (skin on)

1 tablespoon olive oil

12 heads of purple sprouting broccoli

250g live clams, rinsed under cold running water (discard any with damaged shells or open shells that won't close when tapped)

10 cherry tomatoes, halved

2 garlic cloves, thinly sliced

2 teaspoons thyme leaves, chopped

100ml dry white wine

20g mixed pumpkin and sunflower seeds

sea salt and freshly ground black pepper

FOR THE ROMESCO SAUCE

1 large roasted red pepper from a jar

1 garlic clove, smashed

55g blanched almonds, toasted

55g tomato purée

2 tablespoons chopped flat-leaf parsley

2 tablespoons sherry vinegar

1 teaspoon smoked paprika

½ teaspoon cayenne pepper

125ml extra virgin olive oil

I love cooking fish for supper, and it's probably my favourite choice because I grew up on the island of Ireland where you can get some of the best fish in the world. I vary the types of fish I use in this dish – anything that's in season and quite meaty with a skin that will crisp up, such as salmon, sea bass or mackerel. The romesco sauce is fantastic and I would urge you to learn this recipe off by heart, as you can use it as a dip or drizzled over grilled asparagus as a starter or in a pasta dish. Serve with a big leafy green salad.

Preheat the oven to 200°C/gas mark 6.

Place the sea bream fillets, skin-side up, on a baking tray. Brush with the olive oil and season with salt and pepper. Roast for 15 minutes.

While the fish is cooking, make the romesco sauce. Add all the ingredients to a food-processor and process to a thick consistency. Transfer the sauce to a bowl and set aside.

Cook the broccoli in a small quantity of water in a saucepan over a medium heat for about 5–6 minutes until al dente (or longer if you prefer not to have a bite in your stalk), then drain.

Meanwhile, place the clams in another saucepan with the cherry tomatoes, garlic, thyme and wine and cook over a high heat for 10 minutes or until the clams open (discard any that remain closed).

Divide the clams and their cooking juice between four warmed plates and place the roasted sea bream on top. Next place the cooked broccoli in a warmed serving dish, spoon the romesco sauce on top and sprinkle over the pumpkin and sunflower seeds, then serve.

Soda-breaded Bacon Chops with Irish Honey & Whiskey Dip & Colcannon

SERVES 4

2 garlic cloves, crushed

2 small shallots, finely chopped

200g fresh soda breadcrumbs

2 tablespoons Dijon mustard

1 teaspoon thyme leaves

70g plain flour

2 eggs, beaten

4 French-trimmed bacon chops on the bone

50g butter

sea salt and freshly ground black pepper

FOR THE COLCANNON

1kg potatoes, unpeeled and washed

100ml milk

4 spring onions or 100g cabbage, finely chopped

50g butter

¼ teaspoon freshly grated nutmeg

FOR THE IRISH HONEY & WHISKEY DIP

150g clear Irish honey

100ml cider vinegar

100g brown sugar

2 tablespoons Dijon mustard

100ml Irish whiskey

I made this dish a few years back for a party I was hosting at Soho House in New York to celebrate St Patrick's Day. For me it's real comfort food, as I grew up in Ireland, and bacon chops with colcannon were a staple at home. You can use regular fresh white breadcrumbs if you don't have soda bread.

Begin preparing the colcannon. Place the whole potatoes in a large saucepan, with the largest ones at the bottom, and fill the pan halfway with water. Cover the pan with a lid and place over a high heat. When the water begins to boil, drain off about half so that there is just enough left in the pan for the potatoes to steam. Leave to steam, covered, for 30–40 minutes, depending on the size of the potatoes, until soft.

Preheat the oven to 200°C/gas mark 6.

Add the garlic, shallots, breadcrumbs, mustard and thyme leaves to a food-processor. Season with salt and pepper and process for 30 seconds. Transfer the mustard breadcrumb mixture to a bowl. Place the flour and beaten eggs in two separate bowls (or on plates). Dip each bacon chop in the flour, followed by the beaten egg, then turn in the mustard breadcrumb mixture to coat.

Heat an ovenproof frying pan over a high heat and add the butter. Once the butter has melted, place the breaded chops in the pan and brown on each side, then transfer the pan to the oven and cook for 20 minutes.

While the potatoes finish cooking, pour the milk for the colcannon into a saucepan and place over a medium heat. Stir in the spring onions or cabbage, butter and nutmeg, season with salt and pepper and simmer for 4 minutes.

Once the potatoes are cooked, hold them in a tea-towel while you peel them and place in a warmed bowl. Mash the potatoes while you gradually add the warm milk and spring onion or cabbage mixture.

To make the dip, whisk the honey, vinegar and sugar together in a bowl until smooth. Transfer to a saucepan, place over a medium-high heat, stirring constantly to prevent burning, until the mixture begins to boil and thicken. Whisk in the mustard and whiskey and cook for a further minute, continuing to stir constantly. Remove the pan from the heat.

Spoon the colcannon around a large warmed platter, place the breaded bacon chops in the centre, then pour the honey and whiskey dip over the chops.

Hazelnut & Herb-crusted Lamb Cutlets with Pea & Wild Garlic Purée

SERVES 6

The flavours of the herbs and hazelnuts roasted along with the lamb cutlets are utter heaven here, but you could use almonds or pine nuts instead if you prefer. The last time I made this dish was at my good friend and London theatre queen Sally Greene's house. As it was a large supper gathering, I prepared the pea and wild garlic purée ahead in the morning, along with the lamb cutlets right up to the stage of putting them in the oven, so it was very easy to serve. My pan-fried Rosemary Potatoes (see page 39) make a delicious accompaniment.

3 French-trimmed racks of lamb (about 6 cutlets per rack)

2 tablespoons finely chopped mixed rosemary, thyme and flat-leaf parsley

120g blanched hazelnuts, toasted and crushed (see page 156)

2 tablespoons olive oil

sea salt and freshly ground black pepper

FOR THE PEA & WILD GARLIC PURÉE

600g frozen peas

75g wild garlic leaves, thoroughly washed and chopped

75g salted butter

wild garlic flowers and pert leaves, thoroughly washed, to garnish

Remove the racks of lamb from the fridge at least 30 minutes before cooking.

Preheat the oven to 180°C/gas mark 4.

Using a sharp knife, score the fat of the lamb racks in a crisscross pattern. Heat a large frying pan over a high heat. Add each rack in turn, fat side down, to the hot pan and sear the fat, then transfer to a large roasting tin.

Mix the herbs, hazelnuts and olive oil together in a small bowl, then press the mixture onto the seared fat of the lamb racks. Roast for 15 minutes.

While the lamb is roasting, prepare the pea and wild garlic purée. Cook the frozen peas in a saucepan of boiling water for 4 minutes. Drain and add to a blender or food-processor along with the wild garlic and butter. Season with salt and pepper and blend to a smooth consistency. Transfer the purée to a saucepan ready to warm through just before serving.

Remove the lamb racks from the oven and leave to rest for 5 minutes, then slice into individual cutlets. Spoon the warmed pea and wild garlic purée in the centre of four warmed plates and lay three lamb cutlets on top. Garnish each serving with wild garlic flowers and a pert wild garlic leaf.

Lobster Linguine

This is my go-to supper dish for two, when I fancy serving something a little special that doesn't take much time to prepare but still has incredible flavours. When I don't want to splash out on lobster I use Dublin Bay prawns (langoustines), prawns or mussels instead – all are equally delicious!

250g dried linguine

100g unsalted butter

2 shallots, finely diced

1 teaspoon dried chilli flakes

2 garlic cloves, crushed

50ml dry white wine

200g canned cherry tomatoes

2 lobster tails, freshly cooked, shelled and chopped

1 tablespoon chopped flat-leaf parsley

sea salt and freshly ground black pepper

Bring a large saucepan of salted water to the boil over a high heat. Stir in the linguine and keep stirring for the first 2 minutes of cooking – this will stop the pasta from sticking together. Continue to cook the pasta according to the packet instructions until al dente. Drain the pasta, reserving a few tablespoons of the cooking water. Return the cooked pasta to the pan, adding the reserved pasta cooking water to prevent it from clumping together.

While the pasta is cooking, place a frying pan over a medium heat and add the butter. Once the butter is melted, stir in the shallots, chilli flakes and garlic and leave to cook for about a minute.

Add the white wine and cook for about 2 minutes until the alcohol has evaporated. Stir in the canned cherry tomatoes, season with salt and pepper and cook for 1 minute. Then add the chopped lobster meat and parsley and warm through.

Place the saucepan with the pasta over a low heat, stir in the lobster sauce and continue to stir until all the sauce has coated the pasta before serving.

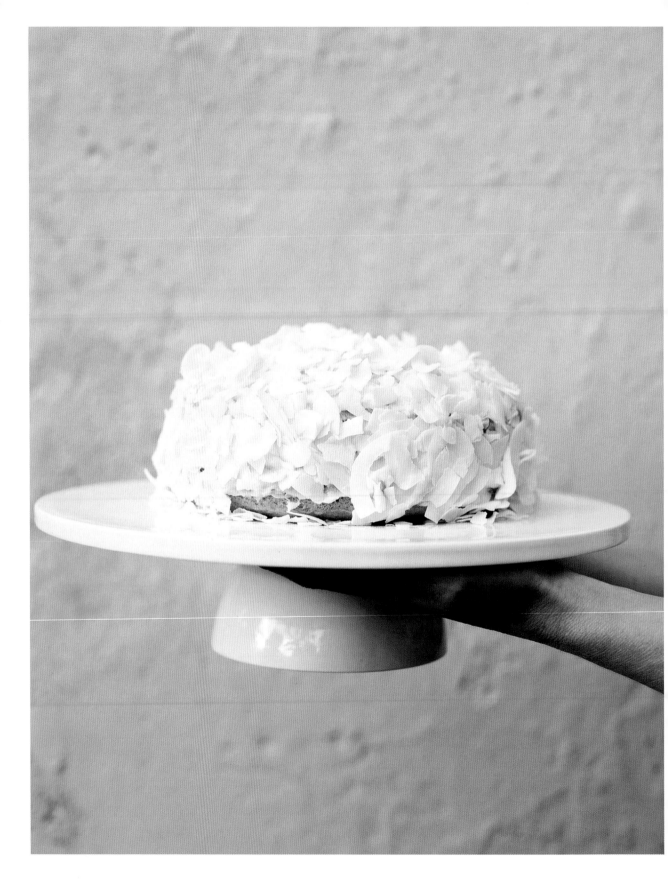

Coconut & Lemon Cloud Cake

MAKES 1 CAKE

A beautifully light, fluffy cake scented with the exotic flavour of coconut and fresh, citrusy lemon, this is the perfect finale for a pungent wild garlic supper to cleanse the palate, although it works equally well as an afternoon or celebration cake. You can use coconut butter instead of dairy butter and/or coconut flour in place of the plain wheat flour. And for convenience, you can make and bake the cake layers a couple of days ahead and then prepare the frosting and assemble the cake on the day you are planning to serve it.

FOR THE CAKE

300g plain flour

1 teaspoon baking powder

1 teaspoon bicarbonate of soda

300g caster sugar

300g unsalted butter, melted, plus extra for greasing

250ml coconut milk

2 eggs

juice of 1 lemon

1 tablespoon coconut oil

1 teaspoon vanilla extract

FOR THE FROSTING

200g unsalted butter, softened

250g icing sugar, sifted

grated zest and juice of 1 lemon

1 teaspoon coconut oil

200g raw coconut flakes, to decorate

Preheat the oven to 180°C/gas mark 4, and lightly grease two 20cm loose-based sandwich tins.

For the cake, sift the flour, baking powder and bicarbonate of soda into a large bowl or the bowl of a stand mixer fitted with the paddle attachment and mix in the sugar. In a separate bowl, combine the melted butter, coconut milk, eggs, lemon juice, coconut oil and vanilla extract and whisk together thoroughly. Then add the wet mixture to the dry mixture and beat together until well combined.

Divide the cake batter evenly between the prepared tins and level the surface with a spatula or the back of a spoon. Bake for about 25 minutes or until well risen and golden.

Remove the cakes from the oven and leave to cool in the tins for about 15 minutes. Then remove them from the tins and transfer to a wire rack to cool completely.

To make the frosting, place all the ingredients in a bowl or the bowl of the stand mixer and use an electric hand mixer or the paddle attachment on the stand mixer to beat on a high speed until light and fluffy.

To assemble, place one of the cakes, top facing downwards, on a cake plate or stand and spread with about one-third of the frosting to cover it. Add the other cake, top facing upwards, and cover the entire cake with the remaining frosting. Sprinkle raw coconut flakes all over the cake to decorate.

Rhubarb, Rosewater & Pistachio Galettes

MAKES 4
GALETTES

FOR THE FILLING

600g rhubarb, trimmed and
cut into 2.5cm pieces on the
diagonal

80g golden caster sugar

2 tablespoons rosewater

FOR THE PASTRY

180g plain flour, plus extra for
dusting

140g unsalted butter, chilled and
cubed

1 tablespoon golden caster sugar

2 tablespoons cold water

FOR GLAZING

1 egg

1 tablespoon milk

1 tablespoon brown sugar

FOR THE PISTACHIO
ROSEWATER MASCARPONE

80g pistachio nuts, chopped

120g mascarpone cheese

1 tablespoon rosewater

Rosewater is one of my favourite flavours as it's delicately fragrant, so do buy a
bottle or two for your store cupboard. Whenever I am roasting rhubarb I add a few
dashes of rosewater, but it's also delicious added to whipped cream, sponge cakes,
raspberries, strawberries – I could go on...

These galettes are so easy to make. Once you have prepared the pastry, it really
is only a matter of spooning the rhubarb in the centre and popping them in the
oven. At other times of the year you can substitute whatever fruits are in season,
such as apples or peaches, for the rhubarb. Last Easter I made one large version of
the galette and it looked amazing on the table.

For the filling, place the rhubarb in a bowl with the caster sugar and toss well
to coat the rhubarb. Then transfer the rhubarb to a sieve or colander set over a
bowl and leave for a couple of hours to release any excess moisture.

To make the pastry, place the flour, butter and sugar in a food-processor and
pulse until you have a breadcrumb consistency. Transfer the mixture to a
large bowl and drizzle over the cold water. Gently mix with your hands until
a dough forms. Turn the dough out onto a lightly floured work surface and
knead it together, pressing to incorporate any dry bits of flour. Flatten the
dough into a disc about 2.5cm thick, wrap in clingfilm and chill in the fridge
at least an hour.

Preheat the oven to 180°C/gas mark 4. Line a baking tray with baking paper.

Tip the rhubarb into a bowl, add the rosewater and toss to combine. In a small
bowl, beat the egg and milk for glazing together. Set both aside while you roll
out the pastry.

Remove the pastry disc from the fridge, unwrap and cut it into four equal
pieces. Roll out one piece of dough on a lightly floured work surface into a
13cm round. Spoon one-quarter of the rhubarb filling into the centre of the
pastry round, leaving a 2.5cm border. Brush the border with the egg wash
and fold the edges of the dough up and over the rhubarb, overlapping slightly.
Brush the border with the egg wash and sprinkle with a little of the brown
sugar. Repeat the process to make the other galettes and transfer them to the
lined baking tray.

Bake for 35–40 minutes until the pastry is golden brown.

For the mascarpone, mix the pistachios, mascarpone and rosewater together
in a small bowl and serve alongside the warm baked galettes.

Guinness Caramel Tiramisu

SERVES 4

Ever since living in Italy a few years back, I have a real soft spot for tiramisu. The Guinness caramel brings a fun twist to the original recipe as well as a delicious depth of flavour, and makes it a great Irish dessert to serve on St Patrick's Day. But you can simply leave out the Guinness if you prefer, or skip the caramel completely for a classic tiramisu.

I like to make my tiramisu in individual vintage cocktail glasses, but you could easily double up the recipe and make it in a glass trifle bowl for a spectacular centrepiece. This is a dessert that you can make ahead the night before.

3 egg yolks

90g caster sugar

400g mascarpone cheese

14 Savoiardi sponge fingers (lady fingers or boudoir biscuits)

100ml cold strong coffee or espresso

120g cocoa powder

FOR THE GUINNESS CARAMEL

180g caster sugar

100ml water

60g unsalted butter

100ml single cream

100ml Guinness

Place the egg yolks and caster sugar in a large bowl and use an electric hand whisk to whisk together until pale and thick. Add the mascarpone and whisk slowly until the mixture is pale and smooth.

To make the Guinness caramel, add the sugar and water to a saucepan, place over a low heat and stir until the sugar has dissolved. Then increase the heat to high and cook for 12–14 minutes or until the syrup is light golden brown in colour. Stir in the butter and cook for a further 2–3 minutes or until the mixture is a caramel consistency. Stir in the cream and Guinness, then reduce the heat and simmer for 10 minutes or until the caramel is a thick consistency.

Dip the sponge fingers into the cold coffee and then place straight into four cocktail glasses to create the base layer. Alternatively, arrange the coffee-dipped sponge fingers in a large glass bowl to make one large tiramisu.

Spoon half the mascarpone mixture over the sponge fingers, followed by a layer of the Guinness caramel and a sprinkle of cocoa and then another layer of the remaining mascarpone mixture and Guinness caramel. Finish with a layer of cocoa on top.

Cover and chill for an hour before serving.

Rhubarb & Crystallised Ginger Upside-down Cake

MAKES 1 CAKE

This cake is one of the easiest to make. It's similar to a tarte tatin in that you caramelise the rhubarb first in an ovenproof frying pan, then pour the batter over and transfer directly to the oven to bake – simple as that! I add crystallised ginger both to the batter and the rhubarb, as it's one of my favourite ingredients and it brings a fantastic sweet yet tangy bite to the cake. You can use other fruits according to the season, such as apples, peaches and pears.

40g unsalted butter

200g soft brown sugar

2 tablepoons finely chopped crystallised ginger

350g rhubarb, trimmed and cut into 2cm pieces

200g plain flour

1 teaspoon baking powder

¼ teaspoon bicarbonate of soda

200ml buttermilk

2 eggs

100ml vegetable oil

crème fraîche, to serve

Preheat the oven to 180°C/gas mark 4.

Melt the butter in a 24cm ovenproof frying pan over a medium heat. Stir in half the sugar and cook for about 2 minutes, then stir in one-third of the crystallised ginger. Remove the pan from the heat and add the rhubarb pieces to cover the base of the pan.

Sift the flour, baking powder and bicarbonate of soda into a bowl.

In a separate bowl, whisk the remaining sugar with the buttermilk, eggs, oil and the remaining crystallised ginger. Fold in the flour mixture and mix well. Pour the batter over the rhubarb and level the surface with a spatula or the back of a spoon.

Bake for 30 minutes or until the cake springs back when you press it in the centre with your fingertip.

Remove the cake from the oven and leave to cool in the pan on a wire rack for 10 minutes. Then invert onto a serving plate and serve with crème fraîche.

Lemon Verbena Possets

SERVES 4

I had kind of forgotten about possets until recently when I was at my favourite Italian restaurant in London, Trullo. They had lemon posset on the dessert menu, which I ordered, served with buttery shortbread for scooping into the posset. It reminded me just how good a posset can be. This recipe is the closest I have come to capturing the Trullo moment. I have added lemon verbena, as it gives it such a delicious lemon depth, but don't worry if you can't find it as you can just leave it out. You can make this dessert up to two days before serving, keeping it in the fridge.

2 lemons

125g caster sugar

6 lemon verbena leaves, plus
4 leaves to serve

425ml double cream

Grate the zest of the lemons into a saucepan, then squeeze out and add the juice, followed by the sugar and lemon verbena leaves.

Place the pan over a low heat and bring to the boil, stirring occasionally until the sugar has dissolved. Whisk in the cream and cook for 3 minutes.

Divide the mixture between four small glasses or ramekins. Leave to cool, then chill in the fridge for 2 hours until set.

Remove the possets from the fridge at least 30 minutes before serving and top each posset with a lemon verbena leaf before serving.

My Italian Baked Ricotta Cheesecake

MAKES 1 CHEESECAKE

I used to make this dessert every couple of weeks when I lived in Turin, Northern Italy, on a square called Piazza Madama Cristina, where there was a daily market that sold the most fantastic lemons from Amalfi. Every time I make it, it takes me back to sunny mornings waking up in my apartment and having an espresso on my balcony while watching all the farmers and vendors setting up their stalls.

I love the savoury sweetness of this baked cheesecake, which is wonderful served with a dollop of crème fraîche scented with lemon zest. When I make it in the summer, I poach summer berries in sugar syrup to serve over the cake. You can prepare and bake the cheesecake up to two days before serving it, keeping it refrigerated in the meantime.

400g ricotta cheese

4 eggs, separated

2 tablespoons plain flour

grated zest and juice of 2 lemons

200g caster sugar

70g butter

12 digestive biscuits, crushed

100g pine nuts, toasted and finely chopped

Preheat the oven to 180°C/gas mark 4.

Place the ricotta in a bowl and whisk in the egg yolks, followed by the flour, lemon zest and juice and sugar, until well combined.

In a separate, very clean and dry bowl, whisk the egg whites until they are stiff and then fold into the ricotta mixture.

Place a saucepan over a low heat and add the butter. Once the butter has melted, remove the pan from the heat and stir in the biscuit crumbs and chopped pine nuts.

Spoon the crumb mixture into a 24cm springform cake tin, using the back of the spoon to spread and press it into an even, well-compacted base.

Pour the lemon ricotta mixture over the base, then bake for 55 minutes.

Remove the cheesecake from the oven. Serve at room temperature or chilled.

Lemon Meringue Pie

MAKES 1 PIE

FOR THE PASTRY

175g plain flour, plus extra for dusting

100g butter, chilled and cubed

1 tablespoon icing sugar

1 egg yolk (reserve the white for the meringue – see below)

1 tablespoon cold water

FOR THE FILLING

1 tablespoon cornflour

grated zest and juice of 2 large lemons

90g golden caster sugar

80g butter, diced

3 egg yolks (reserve the whites for the meringue – see below)

1 egg

FOR THE MERINGUE

4 egg whites, at room temperature

180g golden caster sugar

1 teaspoon cornflour

This is my favourite dessert for serving on a Sunday after a big feast of roast lamb! If you are nervous about making pastry, don't be – just chuck the ingredients in a food-processor, pulse and roll! And you can make it a few days in advance when you have the chance and keep it in the fridge. But if you are stretched for time, use ready-made pastry from the supermarket. The pie is at its best on the day of baking.

First make the pastry. Place all the ingredients in a food-processor and pulse until combined. Turn the dough out onto a lightly floured work surface and knead it together until smooth. Roll out the pastry and use to line a 23cm diameter loose-based fluted flan tin, 2.5cm deep. Trim the excess pastry around the edges and prick the base with a fork. Line the pastry case with a sheet of foil and chill in the fridge for an hour.

Preheat the oven to 180°C/gas mark 4.

Remove the pastry case from the fridge, pour baking beans on top of the foil and bake the pastry case 'blind' for 15 minutes, then leave to cool.

To prepare the filling, mix the cornflour, lemon zest and juice and sugar together in a saucepan. Place over a medium heat and cook, stirring constantly, until thickened. Remove the pan from the heat and whisk in the butter. Beat the egg yolks and whole egg together in a jug, then stir into the pan and return it to a medium heat. Cook, stirring vigorously, for a few minutes until the mixture thickens again. Then remove the pan from the heat and set aside.

To make the meringue, place the egg whites in a very clean and dry large bowl (using a stainless steel one will give you a stiffer meringue) or the bowl of a stand mixer and use an electric hand whisk or the whisk attachment on the stand mixer to whisk until soft peaks form. Gradually add half the sugar, a tablespoon at a time, whisking constantly, then whisk in the cornflour. Finally, add the remaining sugar and whisk until smooth and stiff.

Reheat the filling and then pour it into the pastry case. Immediately add spoonfuls of meringue around the edge of the filling, then spread it so that it just touches the pastry side. Pile the remaining meringue into the centre of the pie, then spread it so that it touches the surface of the hot filling (and starts to cook). Using a knife, swirl the meringue into soft peaks.

Bake for 18–20 minutes until the meringue is crisp and slightly coloured. Remove the pie from the oven and leave to cool in the tin for 30 minutes, then remove it from the tin and leave to cool on a wire rack for a further 30 minutes–1 hour before slicing.

Summer Suppers

Menus

4TH JULY SUPPER

MAPLE & HARISSA CHICKEN WINGS WITH
TABBOULEH

BARBECUED WHISKEY RIBS
WITH SUMMER SLAW

ALL-AMERICAN BERRY TRIFLE

BARBECUE PARTY

SMOKY AUBERGINES WITH MINT
& POMEGRANATE DRESSING

BARBECUED RUMP WITH CHIMICHURRI
& CHARRED CHICORY

BARBECUED PEACHES WITH ROSEMARY
& MAPLE BUTTER

EDIBLE FLOWER SUPPER

COURGETTE BLOSSOMS FILLED WITH
RICOTTA & IRISH HONEY

DANDELION, SAFFRON & SHEEP'S
CHEESE RISOTTO

SWEET GERANIUM CHEESECAKE

SUMMER GARDEN SUPPER

GAZPACHO WITH CUCUMBER & DILL
SALSA

LEMON, HARISSA & OLIVE SPATCHCOCK
CHICKEN WITH BULGAR WHEAT,
CUCUMBER & DILL

ORANGE BLOSSOM SUMMER SPONGE
WITH CREAM & STRAWBERRIES

SUMMER GATHERING

BEETROOT, BLOOD ORANGE
& GIN-CURED SALMON
WITH FENNEL & DILL PICKLE

SEAFOOD PAELLA

RASPBERRY & ROSEWATER PAVLOVA

WEST CORK FORAGED SUPPER

NETTLE SOUP WITH SEAWEED SCONES

WHOLE BAKED SEA BASS WITH HERBS,
LEMON & BUTTERED PURSLANE

CARRAGEEN MOSS PUDDINGS WITH
CARRAGEEN FRITTERS

WILD SALMON SUPPER

DUBLIN BAY PRAWNS PIL PIL WITH
DIPPING TOASTS

WHOLE POACHED WILD SALMON
WITH FRESH HORSERADISH CREAM
& NEW POTATO SALAD

WATERMELON & MINT GRANITA

Nettle Soup with Seaweed Scones

SERVES 4

50g butter

350g potatoes, peeled and diced

1 onion, diced

800ml hot vegetable stock

200g young nettle leaves and tender stalks, thoroughly washed

½ teaspoon freshly grated nutmeg

100ml double cream

sea salt and freshly ground black pepper

clover blossoms, thoroughly washed, to garnish

FOR THE SEAWEED SCONES

15g dulse, finely chopped (you could also use other varieties, such as kelp)

225g plain flour, plus extra for dusting

1 tablespoon baking powder

pinch of fine sea salt

50g butter, chilled and cubed

125–150ml buttermilk, plus extra for brushing

vegetable oil, for oiling

Nettles grow wild everywhere, so it's easy to forage for them – just wear rubber gloves! Pick the small leaves at the top as they are the sweetest and fret not – once they are dropped in boiling water they lose their sting. Nettles are incredibly good for you, as they are packed with iron. The taste is similar to spinach, but more interesting and sweeter. The seaweed scones add a delicious saltiness to the dish. If you don't want to use seaweed in the scones then rosemary, thyme or dried oregano would be delicious instead.

Place a heavy-based saucepan over a medium heat and add the butter. Once the butter has melted, add the potatoes and onion, stir well and cover the pan with a lid. Reduce the heat to low and leave the vegetables to sweat for about 10 minutes, stirring occasionally.

Pour in the hot stock, increase the heat to high and cook, uncovered, for about 10 minutes until the potatoes and onion are completely soft.

Using gloves, add the nettles (they lose their sting once cooked) and nutmeg, stir and cook for 2–3 minutes until the nettles have wilted.

Transfer the soup to a blender or food-processor, or use a hand blender, and blend to a smooth consistency.

Return the soup to the saucepan (if necessary) and season. Stir in the cream and place over a medium heat for just 2 minutes to warm through.

Meanwhile, make the scones. Preheat the oven to 200°C/gas mark 6.

Spread the dulse out on a baking tray and roast in the oven for 2 minutes, then remove from the oven.

Sift the flour, baking powder and salt into a large bowl. Add the butter and rub in with your fingertips until the mixture resembles fine breadcrumbs.

Stir the dulse into the mixture, then gradually mix in enough buttermilk with a fork to make a soft dough. Roll out the dough on a floured work surface to a thickness of 1cm. Cut into rounds using a 7.5cm pastry cutter or an upturned glass. Oil the baking tray used for the dulse, place the rounds on the tray and brush with buttermilk. Bake for 12–15 minutes until golden brown. Transfer the scones to a wire rack and leave to cool for 10 minutes before serving.

Serve the soup in warmed bowls, garnished with clover blossoms, along with the warm seaweed scones.

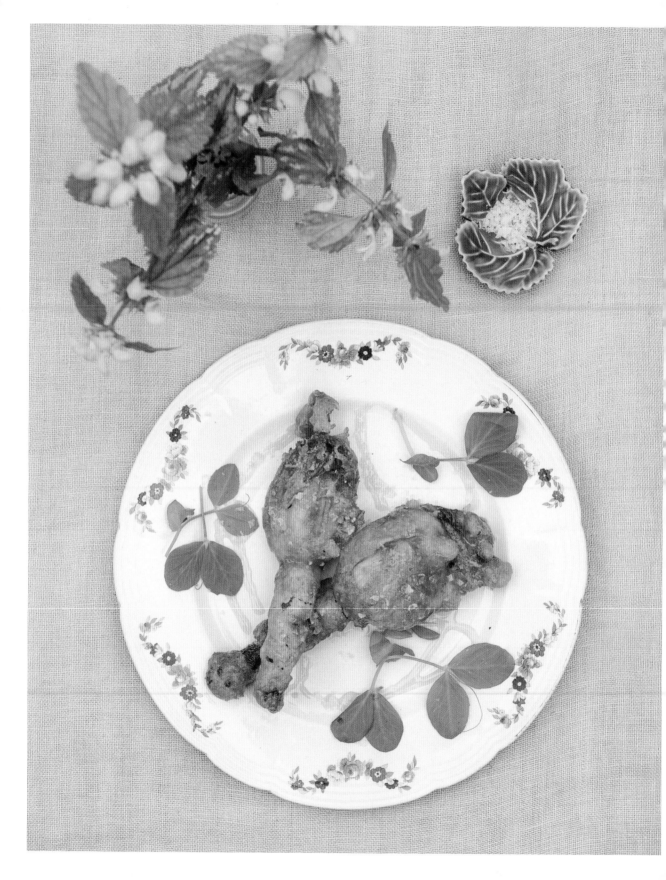

Courgette Blossoms Filled with Ricotta & Irish Honey

SERVES 4

My all-time favourite summer starter– crisp blossoms filled with light and creamy honeyed ricotta. I use beautiful wild Irish honey or you can source a good local honey – it will make a world of difference to the flavour of the dish. I sometimes serve this as a main course with grilled courgettes circled around the plate. The best tip I can pass on for when you are cooking these, is to ensure you twist the top of the courgette blossom and hold onto it as you are dropping each one into the batter and then the oil. This will help it from breaking apart when frying. You can get the filling made the day ahead and then fill the courgette blossoms on the day you plan to cook them.

200g ricotta cheese

2 tablespoons chopped mint

80ml clear Irish honey

12 courgette flowers

200ml vegetable oil

80g pea shoots

sea salt

FOR THE BATTER

200g plain flour

2 teaspoons bicarbonate of soda

400ml soda water

For the filling, beat the ricotta in a bowl until soft and smooth, then stir in the mint and honey. Carefully scoop the filling into the courgette flowers – you should be able to fit 2–4 teaspoons in each one, depending on their size. Twist the petals gently to enclose the mixture.

Just before you are ready to cook, prepare the batter. Sift the flour and bicarbonate of soda together into a bowl, then lightly whisk in the soda water until you have a batter with the consistency of single cream. Be careful not to over-whisk, so don't worry if there are a few lumps of flour remaining.

Heat the vegetable oil in a deep saucepan to 180–190°C or until a cube of bread browns in 30 seconds.

Dip one stuffed courgette flower into the batter and immediately lower into the hot oil, then repeat with a couple more – don't cook more than three or four at a time. Deep-fry for 1–2 minutes until puffed up, crisp and golden brown. Remove from the oil and drain on kitchen paper while you fry the remaining stuffed flowers. Season with salt.

To serve, arrange the fried courgette flowers on a plate and sprinkle the pea shoots around them.

Dublin Bay Prawns Pil Pil with Dipping Toasts

SERVES 6

I remember the first time that I ever had prawns pil pil, it was in the famous Boqueria market in Barcelona. I sat at the counter of one of the tapas bars, and watched how they fired up the plump fresh prawns with fiery chillies, aromatic garlic and smoky paprika. They were out of this world... They served them with very thinly sliced sourdough toasts that were brushed with olive oil. I scooped the prawns pil pil onto the toasts to create the perfect bite! It is one of the easiest and fastest starters that I know. I also make them when I want a late-night supper that's light but bursting with flavour.

100ml olive oil

6 garlic cloves, sliced

1 teaspoon dried chilli flakes

30 raw Dublin Bay prawns (langoustines), peeled and deveined (see page 33) but tails left intact

2 teaspoons smoked paprika

1 tablespoon dry sherry

juice of 1 lemon

1 tablespoon chopped flat-leaf parsley

sea salt and freshly ground black pepper

sourdough toasts, to serve

Place a frying pan over a medium heat and add the olive oil, followed by the garlic and chilli flakes. Cook for 2 minutes.

Toss in the Dublin Bay prawns, followed by the smoked paprika, dry sherry and lemon juice, and season with salt and pepper. Cook for a further 5 minutes. Just before you take the pan off the heat, toss in the parsley.

Serve with sourdough toasts for scooping up all the juices.

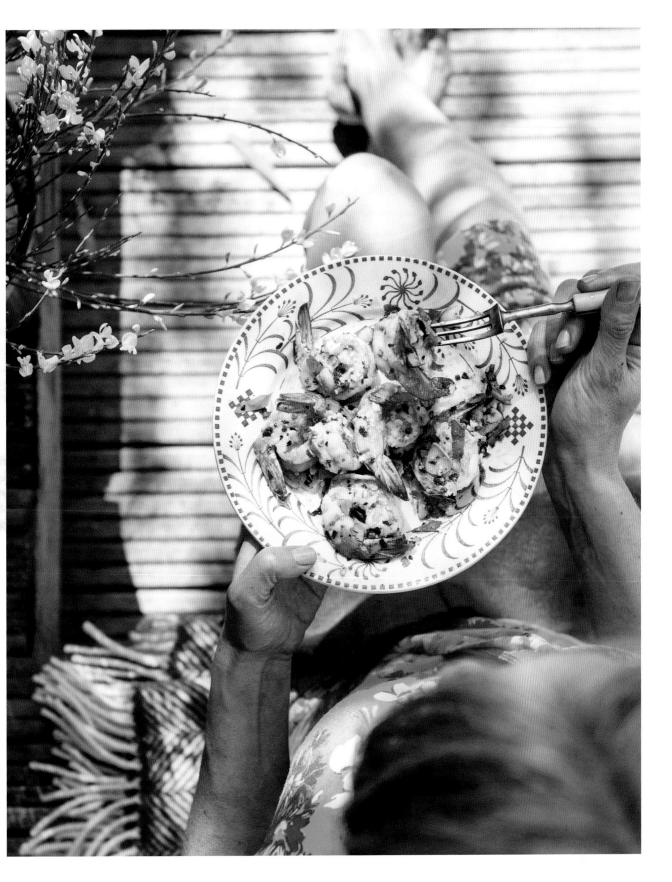

Smoky Aubergines with Mint & Pomegranate Dressing

SERVES 6

I just love the flavour of smoked aubergines. When I am not using the barbecue, I smoke the aubergines by placing them over a gas flame, turning every few minutes, to blacken the skin. Do this for about 15 minutes until the aubergine collapses, or grill them on a hot griddle pan. The dressing is so delicious with the smoky aubergines, and do sprinkle extra pomegranate seeds and chopped fresh mint on top before you serve, as it will look so pretty.

2 aubergines, sliced

2 tablespoons olive oil

sea salt and freshly ground black pepper

FOR THE MINT & POMEGRANATE DRESSING

200ml Greek yogurt

2 tablespoons chopped mint

1 tablespoon tahini

juice of ½ lemon

1 pomegranate

Lay the aubergine slices on a rack and lightly sprinkle the exposed sides with salt, then leave for 10 minutes until you see beads of water come to the surface. Dry the aubergine slices off with kitchen paper, then turn them over and repeat the process. This stops the aubergines from tasting bitter.

Prepare a charcoal barbecue or heat a gas barbecue to a high heat, or place a griddle pan over a high heat. Brush the aubergine slices with the olive oil and grill on each side for 3 minutes.

Meanwhile, make the dressing. Whisk all the ingredients except the pomegranate together in a bowl and season with salt and pepper. Cut the pomegranate in half and then, holding each half in turn, cut-side down, over the dressing bowl, use the back of a wooden spoon to firmly tap the skin side of the pomegranate so that the seeds fall directly into the dressing. Mix the pomegranate seeds into the dressing.

Place the grilled aubergines on a serving platter and drizzle the dressing over the top.

Gazpacho with Cucumber & Dill Salsa

SERVES 6

This is so easy to make as it's really just a case of chopping and blending. The key thing is that you use very ripe tomatoes that are full of flavour. The best way to ripen tomatoes is to place them in a brown paper bag with a banana. It sounds odd but it works! And never store tomatoes in the fridge, as they won't ripen properly. I try to make this soup a day ahead and keep it in my fridge. It should be served very chilled. The cucumber and dill salsa adds great texture, and you could also add some croûtons on top if you wish. When I am having lots of people over for a party, I serve the gazpacho in small glasses.

1kg very ripe tomatoes, diced

100g slightly stale crusty white or sourdough bread, torn into pieces

2 red peppers, cored, deseeded and diced

1 cucumber, diced

2 spring onions, chopped

3 garlic cloves, crushed

2 tablespoons sherry vinegar

200ml extra virgin olive oil

sea salt and freshly ground black pepper

FOR THE SALSA

½ cucumber, diced

2 tablespoons chopped dill

2 tablespoons extra virgin olive oil

Place the tomatoes, bread, red peppers, cucumber, spring onions, garlic, sherry vinegar and olive oil in a blender or food-processor and season with salt and pepper. Blend the ingredients until smooth.

Transfer the mixture to a bowl, cover with clingfilm and chill in the fridge for an hour.

To make the salsa, mix all the ingredients together in a bowl.

To serve, pour the gazpacho into bowls and spoon the salsa on top.

Beetroot, Blood Orange & Gin-cured Salmon with Fennel & Dill Pickle

SERVES 4

I developed this recipe for a theatre supper that I was cooking at my friend Sally Greene's house in London. The colours are simply dazzling on the plate and this is a really fabulous first course for when you want to get a head start, as you have to prepare it a couple of days beforehand to allow it to cure. If you can't get hold of blood oranges, then just use regular oranges. If you want to slice it before your guests arrive, ensure you wrap it tight in clingfilm so that it doesn't dry out.

FOR THE SALMON

300g salmon side fillet

100g peeled raw beetroot, grated

30g granulated sugar

20g sea salt

1 tablespoon finely chopped dill

grated zest and juice of 1 small blood orange

2 tablespoons gin

FOR THE FENNEL & DILL PICKLE

1 fennel bulb

80g granulated sugar

1 tablespoon finely chopped dill

1 teaspoon sea salt

250ml cider vinegar

1 blood orange, sliced, to decorate (optional)

Start by preparing the salmon, as you will need to let this cure for a couple of days. Place the salmon, skin-side down, in a dish that's deep enough for it to be submerged in the cure – I find a baking or pie dish is perfect. Add all the remaining ingredients for the salmon to a bowl and mix together well. Spoon over the salmon so that the salmon is submerged in the cure. Cover the dish loosely with two sheets of clingfilm and sit a heavy weight on top – I use cans of tomatoes or similar canned items. Place in the fridge and leave for two days.

Next make the fennel and dill pickle. Cut the fennel bulb in half down the centre and thinly slice into semicircles. Add to a non-reactive bowl, sprinkle over the sugar, dill and salt and pour the vinegar on top. Cover the bowl with clingfilm and leave to stand at room temperature for about an hour. Give the pickle a good stir and then leave to stand for a further hour.

Once the salmon has cured for two days, remove from the fridge, scrape off all the cure mixture and pat the salmon dry with kitchen paper.

To serve, thinly slice the salmon away from the skin underneath and arrange on a serving plate with slices of blood orange, if you wish, and the fennel and dill pickle in a bowl alongside.

Maple & Harissa Chicken Wings with Tabbouleh

SERVES 6

Sticky, sweet and spicy chicken wings, scooped up with a fresh tabbouleh – utterly delicious!
You can leave out the tabbouleh if you just want to serve the chicken wings as finger food. This is
perfect barbecue food, and you can get them marinated a day in advance for an extra depth
of flavour and to tenderise the chicken.

120g bulgar wheat or couscous

125ml boiling water

100ml maple syrup

6 garlic cloves, crushed

2 tablespoons harissa

1.5kg organic or free-range
chicken wings, tips removed

1 bunch each of mint, coriander
and flat-leaf parsley, leaves
picked

100g rocket leaves

2 spring onions, thinly sliced
lengthways

1 cucumber, diced

2 teaspoons sumac

juice of 1 lemon

80ml extra virgin olive oil

sea salt and freshly ground black
pepper

Prepare a charcoal barbecue or heat a gas barbecue to a high heat, or preheat
the oven to 220°C/gas mark 7.

Place the bulgar wheat (or couscous) in a heatproof bowl and pour over the
boiling water to cover. Cover the bowl with clingfilm and leave to soak for
about 20 minutes or until all the water is absorbed, then fluff up with a fork.

Mix the maple syrup, three-quarters of the garlic, 1 tablespoon of the harissa
and a large pinch of salt together in a large bowl. Add the chicken wings and
toss to coat in the mixture, then arrange in a single layer on a baking tray.

Roast on the hot barbecue or in the oven for 45 minutes or until caramelised
and golden and cooked through, turning halfway through, then toss with the
remaining tablespoon of harissa.

While the chicken wings are roasting, finish preparing the tabbouleh. Mix the
herbs, rocket, spring onions and cucumber with the bulgar wheat.

Whisk the sumac, lemon juice, extra virgin olive oil and remaining garlic
together in a small bowl and season with salt and pepper. Add the dressing to
the tabbouleh and toss to coat.

Serve the caramelised wings with the tabbouleh.

Dandelion, Saffron & Sheep's Cheese Risotto

SERVES 4

50g butter

2 shallots, very finely chopped

2 garlic cloves, crushed

300g Arborio (risotto) rice

100ml dry white wine

500ml hot vegetable or chicken stock

½ teaspoon saffron threads

100g soft crumbly sheep's cheese, such as feta, crumbled

50g mascarpone cheese

80g dandelion leaves, thoroughly washed

sea salt and freshly ground black pepper

I developed this recipe a few years back when I was doing a takeover at Cheyne Walk Brasserie in London for the Chelsea Flower Show. Every dish on the menu was infused with beautiful edible flowers so, as you can imagine, it was such an exciting menu to create! The dandelions look so pretty in the risotto but they are a little bitter so the addition of the saffron balances out the dish with its smoky sweet flavour. I have also used courgette flowers in this risotto instead of the dandelions.

Place a saucepan over a medium heat and add the butter. When the butter has melted, stir in the shallots and garlic, then cover the pan with a lid, reduce the heat and leave to sweat for about 2 minutes until the shallots are softened but not browned.

Stir in the rice and toast for about 1 minute until it is dry. Pour in the wine, stir and cook for about 2 minutes until almost all of it has been absorbed.

Add the hot stock, a ladleful at a time, stirring constantly. Wait until the stock has been fully absorbed before adding the next ladleful. It should take 15–20 minutes for all the stock to be absorbed and the rice to be cooked, but check by tasting as you go.

About 2 minutes before the rice is cooked, stir in the saffron. After a further minute stir in the sheep's cheese and mascarpone, continue to cook for a further minute before serving. Season with salt and pepper.

Remove the pan from the heat and stir in the dandelion leaves, then divide the risotto between warmed bowls.

Barbecued Rump with Chimichurri & Charred Chicory

SERVES 6

I absolutely love the flavours of chimichurri – it adds a massive burst of freshness, heat and saltiness to the beef. You can use it with chicken, meaty fish, lamb or pork or over halloumi. The charred chicory is delicious cooked on the barbecue, I also love radicchio cooked the same way. If you are looking for a good salad to go along with this dish then my Bulgar Wheat Salad on page 80 works perfectly.

800g rump steak in one piece

3 heads of white chicory

good-quality extra virgin olive oil, for drizzling

sea salt and freshly ground black pepper

FOR THE CHIMICHURRI

1 bunch of flat-leaf parsley, roughly chopped

4 tablespoons chopped mint

1 tablespoooon chopped thyme leaves

2 garlic cloves, crushed

2 anchovy fillets, chopped

2 green chillies, deseeded and sliced

100ml white wine vinegar

2 tablespoons olive oil

1 tablespoon clear Irish honey

First make the chimichurri. Add all the ingredients to a food-processor and pulse until roughly chopped. Transfer to a bowl and set aside.

Prepare a charcoal barbecue or heat a gas barbecue to a high heat, or place a griddle pan over a high heat. Sprinkle the steak with salt and pepper and grill for 3 minutes on each side for medium-rare. Set aside and keep warm.

Grill the chicory for 1 minute on each side or until golden. Remove from the barbecue or pan, then drizzle with extra virgin olive oil and season with salt and pepper.

Thinly slice the steak, spoon over the chimichurri and serve with the grilled chicory.

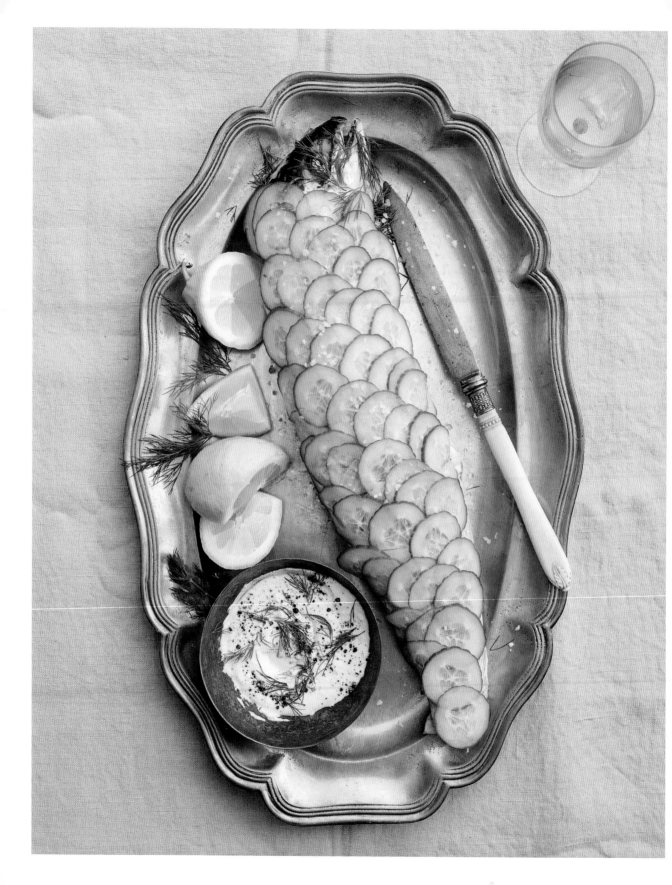

Whole Poached Wild Salmon with Fresh Horseradish Cream & New Potato Salad

SERVES 10

1 whole salmon, about 2.5kg, scaled and cleaned

3 bay leaves

3 fennel sprigs

2 lemons, cut into wedges

1 teaspoon whole black peppercorns

½ cucumber

5 fennel sprigs

FOR THE NEW POTATO SALAD

1.8kg new potatoes or Jersey Royals, washed

6 tablespoons torn mint leaves

100g salted butter

4 shallots, finely diced

grated zest and juice of 2 lemons

2 teaspoons Dijon mustard

40 fresh pea pods, podded, or 200g frozen peas

20 radishes, finely sliced

sea salt and freshly ground black pepper

FOR THE HORSERADISH CREAM

20cm piece of horseradish root, peeled and grated

150ml crème fraîche

juice of 1 lemon

The horseradish cream is peppery and utterly delicious with the salmon but I sometimes serve this with a pistachio yogurt instead – simply mix finely chopped pistachios with natural yogurt and season well. The potato salad is also lovely alongside roasts or barbecues. Add a couple of tablespoons of crème fraîche if you want a creamier salad, and it's just as good if you make it a day ahead of serving.

Place the salmon in a fish kettle and pour over enough cold water to cover the whole fish. Add the bay leaves, fennel sprigs, half thelemon wedges and peppercorns. Bring to the boil, then turn off the heat and leave the salmon to cool completely in the water.

For the potato salad, place the potatoes in a saucepan half-filled with water and add 1 tablespoon of the mint and a sprinkle of salt. Cover the pan with a lid and bring to the boil over a high heat. Cook for 20–25 minutes or until the potatoes are completely cooked through but still firm.

While the potatoes are cooking, place a frying pan over a medium heat and add the butter. Once the butter is melted, add the shallots and cook for about 5 minutes or until soft. Remove the pan from the heat, stir in the lemon zest and juice and mustard, season with salt and pepper and set aside.

Drain the potatoes, then slice them in half and add them to your serving dish, followed by the fresh peas. If you are using frozen peas, cook them in a pan of salted boiling water for 2–3 minutes, then drain well and add to the potatoes.

Add the radishes, the remaining fresh mint and the lemon butter to the potatoes. Toss together so all the ingredients are completely coated.

Drain the salmon, leaving it to drain free of any remaining liquid. Using a paring knife or your fingers, carefully remove the skin from the salmon and discard. Transfer the salmon to a serving platter.

For the horseradish cream, add all the ingredients to a small bowl and mix together well.

For the garnish, very thinly slice the cucumber and arrange the slices along the centre of the fish. Then garnish the rim of the salmon with the fennel sprigs and the remaining lemon wedges and serve with the potato salad and horseradish cream alongside.

Lemon, Harissa & Olive Spatchcock Chicken with Bulgar Wheat, Cucumber & Dill

SERVES 6

Spatchcock chicken is a really great way to get lots of flavours right into the chicken. You can do it yourself or otherwise ask your butcher to do it for you. The combination of the zesty lemons, sweet and smoky harissa and earthy olive is so Mediterranean. I also use this recipe with meaty fish, like hake or cod. The bulgar wheat is so refreshing and works perfectly alongside the chicken.

1 whole organic or free-range chicken, about 1.4kg

2 preserved lemons, chopped

6 garlic cloves, smashed

50g pitted black olives, chopped

1 tablespoon harissa

100ml olive oil

sea salt and freshly ground black pepper

FOR THE BULGAR
WHEAT SALAD

100g bulgar wheat

100ml boiling water

1 cucumber, diced

4 spring onions, thinly sliced

2 tablespoons chopped flat-leaf parsley

2 tablespoons chopped dill

1 tablespoon chopped mint

100ml extra virgin olive oil

juice of 1 lemon

3 garlic cloves, crushed

Preheat the oven to 180°C/gas mark 4.

To spatchcock the chicken, place it breast-side down, with the legs towards you. Using sturdy scissors, cut along either side of the backbone to remove it, cutting through the rib bones as you go. Open the chicken out and turn it over. Flatten the breastbone with the heel of your hand so that the meat is all one thickness. You can ask your butcher to do this for you if you prefer.

Add the preserved lemons, garlic, olives, harissa and olive oil to a bowl and mix together well.

Place the spatchcocked chicken in a roasting tray and rub the preserved lemon and harissa mixture all over the chicken. Season with salt and pepper. Roast for 45 minutes or until cooked through. To check if the chicken is cooked, insert a skewer into the thickest part of the thigh – the juices should run clear.

While the chicken is roasting, prepare the bulgar wheat salad. Place the bulgar in a heatproof bowl and pour over the boiling water to cover. Cover the bowl with clingfilm and leave to soak for about 20 minutes or until all the water is absorbed. Fluff up with a fork, then stir in the cucumber, spring onions and herbs. Whisk the oil, lemon juice and garlic together in a small bowl and season with salt and pepper. Add the dressing to the bulgar wheat salad and toss to coat.

Transfer the roast spatchcocked chicken to the centre of a large, warmed platter and spoon the bulgar wheat salad around the chicken to serve.

Whole Baked Sea Bass with Herbs, Lemon & Buttered Purslane

SERVES 4

This is my favourite way to cook and eat fish all year round. Cooking fish on the bone brings so much flavour, and with just a sprinkle of aromatic herbs, zesty lemon juice and a drizzle of extra virgin olive oil – it's the best way to cook fresh sea bass. Once cooked, sprinkle with fresh herbs, lemon juice and extra virgin olive oil. I like to serve a large bowl of lightly dressed salad leaves with the fish, as well as the purslane, but nothing too heavy as it should be all about the simple flavours enhancing this beautiful fish. I also love cooking fish like this on the barbecue.

4 whole sea bass, scaled and cleaned

4 flat-leaf parsley sprigs

4 mint sprigs

4 lemons, sliced, plus 1 for squeeezing

50g butter

200g purslane, thoroughly washed

4 tablespoons chopped mixed flat-leaf parsley, mint and basil

extra virgin olive oil, for drizzling

sea salt and freshly ground black pepper

Preheat the oven to 200°C/gas mark 6.

Lay the sea bass on a baking tray. Add a parsley and mint sprig to the cavity of each fish, along with a sliced lemon. Season with salt and pepper. Bake for 20 minutes.

While the fish finishes baking, place a frying pan over a medium heat and add the butter. Once it has melted, add the purslane, season with salt and pepper and cook, tossing, for 3 minutes.

Remove the sea bass from the oven. Gently lift away and discard the skin, and trim any fat from around the fish. Transfer each fish to a warmed plate. Sprinkle the chopped herbs on top, drizzle with extra virgin olive oil and add a squeeze of lemon, then season with salt and pepper. Serve with the buttered purslane.

Barbecued Whiskey Ribs with Summer Slaw

SERVES 6

2kg pork belly rib racks

FOR THE MARINADE

150ml clear Irish honey

150ml sweet soy sauce

150ml Irish whiskey

10cm piece of fresh ginger,
peeled and grated

1 teaspoon sesame oil

½ teaspoon ground cinnamon

sea salt and freshly ground black
pepper

FOR THE SUMMER SLAW

100ml mayonnaise

2 tablespoons finely chopped
flat-leaf parsley

½ green cabbage, cored and cut
into strips

2 celery sticks, thinly sliced

2 carrots, peeled and grated

juice of 1 lemon

These ribs are smoky, sweet and made punchy with the fresh ginger – along with the fresh summer slaw it's such a fabulous barbecue dish. Get the ribs marinated a day ahead so that they have time to infuse the pork. You can leave the whiskey out of the marinade if you want, and there's no need to replace it with anything. This marinade also works really well with pork chops and chicken pieces. The slaw can also be made the day before so it's all quite stress free!

Whisk all the ingredients for the marinade together in a bowl.

Place the rib racks in a roasting tray and pour over the marinade, turning to coat them all over. Cover loosely with clingfilm and leave to marinate in the fridge for 4 hours (or overnight if possible).

Preheat the oven to 140°C/gas mark 1.

Remove the rib racks from the fridge, uncover and drain off the excess marinade into a bowl. Baste the ribs with some of the excess marinade, then cover the roasting tray with foil and roast for 4 hours or until the meat is falling off the bone, basting every so often with more marinade.

Remove the roasting tray from the oven and cut the rib racks between the bones into individual ribs. Increase the oven temperature to 220°C/gas mark 7, or prepare a charcoal barbecue or heat a gas barbecue to a high heat.

Meanwhile, to make the summer slaw, toss all the ingredients together in a large serving bowl and season with salt and pepper. Cover the bowl with clingfilm and leave in the fridge for an hour before serving.

Pour the remaining marinade into a small saucepan and bring to the boil, then reduce the heat and simmer for about 15 minutes until it is syrupy. Paint the ribs with the reduced marinade and return them to the hot oven or barbecue.

Cook the ribs for about 10 minutes, then turn them over, paint with the remaining reduced marinade and cook for a final 5–7 minutes until sticky and dark.

Serve the ribs with the summer slaw.

Seafood Paella

I love serving a seafood paella at home for supper with my friends – one big pan set in the middle of the table for everyone to enjoy. You can make it up to step two a few hours before serving it – just so that you're not chained to the stove when your guests arrive. There are so many alternative fish that you can use instead of the monkfish, the only thing is that they need to be meaty, so fish like hake and cod also work very well. If you don't have any saffron then use 2 teaspoons of smoked paprika. Serve with a big, green leafy salad.

1kg live mussels

olive oil, for cooking

10cm piece of fully cured, ready-to-eat chorizo, diced

2 onions, diced

2 red peppers, cored, deseeded and sliced

4 garlic cloves, crushed

800g paella rice

1 teaspoon saffron threads

1 litre hot fish stock

500g monkfish fillets, cut into 2–3cm pieces

10 raw prawns in their shells

sea salt and freshly ground black pepper

2 lemons, cut into wedges, to serve

First prepare the mussels. Rinse them under cold running water, then scrub the shells to remove any barnacles and pull away and discard any stringy beards. Discard any with damaged shells or open shells that won't close when tapped.

Heat a large paella pan over a medium heat. Add a splash of olive oil, followed by the chorizo. Cook for about 5 minutes until crisp.

Add the onions, red peppers and garlic to the paella pan and cook for a further 10 minutes, stirring frequently.

Stir in the rice and season with salt and pepper. Add the saffron threads and hot stock and leave to simmer for about 15 minutes.

Scatter the pieces of monkfish over the rice and push under the surface with the back of a spoon. Lay the mussels and prawns over the top and simmer for a further 10 minutes or until all the mussels have opened (discard any that remain closed) and the prawns have turned pink.

Serve the paella in the pan, with the lemon wedges placed around the edge.

Watermelon & Mint Granita

SERVES 6

This is the easiest dessert to make during summer and the most refreshing – so it goes perfectly after a fish main course, to cleanse the palate. I sometimes use fresh basil instead of the mint, which adds a delicious sweetness.

1 medium watermelon, about 3kg

juice of ½ lemon

50g icing sugar, sifted

2 tablespoons finely chopped mint leaves

Cut the melon into wedges, then scrape out the seeds with a teaspoon.

Scoop the pink watermelon flesh into a food-processor and pulse until you have a slush. Transfer the watermelon slush to a fine sieve over a bowl and push it through the sieve using the back of a spoon to create the juice.

Whisk the lemon juice and icing sugar into the watermelon juice, then stir in the mint.

Pour the watermelon mixture into a baking tray or shallow baking tin and place in the freezer. After 30 minutes, remove from the freezer and stir well. Return to the freezer and repeat the process about three more times or until the granita has frozen – about 2 hours in total.

Scoop the granita into chilled glasses to serve.

Raspberry & Rosewater Pavlova

MAKES I PAVLOVA

This is my all-time favourite summer dessert! It is so decadent in flavour and looks absolutely fabulous – everyone loves it! I love the flavour of rosewater and its gentle floral taste works perfectly with the light and fluffy pavlova. I also make the pavlova the evening before and leave it to cool overnight in the oven (after it's turned off). This dish is also delicious with strawberries or peaches when they are in season.

FOR THE RASPBERRY SYRUP

100g fresh raspberries

1 tablespoon caster sugar

FOR THE MERINGUE

9 egg whites, at room temperature

500g caster sugar

2 teaspoons cornflour

1 teaspoon white wine vinegar

1 tablespoon rosewater

FOR THE FILLING

500ml whipping cream

1 tablespoon icing sugar

1 tablespoon rosewater

200g fresh raspberries

Preheat the oven to 160°C/gas mark 3, and line a baking tray with greaseproof paper.

First make the syrup. Combine the raspberries and sugar in a small saucepan, place over a low heat and stir until the sugar has completely dissolved. Cook for a further 2–3 minutes until the raspberries have turned to mush. Transfer the raspberries to a sieve over a bowl and push them through the sieve using the back of a spoon to create a thick, syrup-like consistency. Leave to cool.

To make the meringue, place the egg whites in a very clean and dry large bowl or the bowl of a stand mixer and use an electric hand whisk or the whisk attachment on the stand mixer to whisk until firm peaks form. Gradually add the caster sugar, a tablespoon at a time, whisking constantly until the mixture is thick and glossy and the sugar has completely dissolved. Then add the cornflour, vinegar and rosewater and gently fold in until just combined.

Spoon the meringue onto the lined baking tray to form a round and use the back of a wooden spoon to shape the meringue into a nest. Using a teaspoon, drizzle half the raspberry syrup around the meringue to create a ripple effect.

Place the meringue in the oven, reduce the oven temperature to 140°C/gas mark 1, and bake for 1½ hours. Then turn off the oven, open the oven door and leave the meringue to cool completely.

When the meringue has cooled and you are ready to serve, start assembling the filling – you don't want to add it too far in advance, as it will soak into the meringue. Gently whip the cream in a bowl until it thickens and then whisk in the icing sugar. Fold in the rosewater. Spoon the filling into the centre of the meringue, arrange the fresh raspberries on top and drizzle over the remaining raspberry syrup.

Carrageen Moss Puddings with Carrageen Fritters

SERVES 4

Carrageen moss is a seaweed but it's not strong in flavour, more a gentle taste of the sea as well as a fantastic natural setting agent. The texture of these puddings is so fluffy and creamy. I use the leftover carrageen leaves for fritters – just dry them off, dip them in the batter and fry, which you can do a day ahead. The best place to find carrageen moss is in health food stores or online – you only need a little, so a bag will go a long way. The pudding itself can also be made a day ahead and is simply delicious served with just a spoon of softly whipped cream and a sprinkle of brown sugar.

5g dried carrageen moss (Irish moss)

460ml milk

2½ tablespoons caster sugar

1 vanilla pod

1 egg, separated

FOR THE FRITTERS

130ml buttermilk

1 egg

1 tablespoon caster sugar, plus 35g for coating

80g plain flour

1 teaspoon baking powder

200ml vegetable oil

½ teaspoon ground cinnamon

Soak the carrageen moss in a bowl of lukewarm water for 15 minutes. Drain and place in a saucepan with the milk, 1 tablespoon of the sugar and the vanilla pod. Bring to the boil, then reduce the heat and simmer for 30 minutes or until the mixture has thickened to the consistency of yogurt.

Transfer the mixture to a sieve set over a bowl and push the natural gelatine from the carrageen moss through the sieve with the back of a spoon. Don't discard the cooked carrageen moss, as you will be using it for the fritters, so rinse it under cold water and set aside.

Place the egg yolk in a bowl and whisk in the remaining 1½ tablespoons of sugar, then whisk in the strained milk mixture.

Place the egg white in a very clean and dry bowl and whisk until stiff, then fold into the milk mixture with a metal spoon. Divide the pudding mixture between four small pots and chill in the fridge for about an hour or until set.

To make the carrageen moss fritters, add the buttermilk, egg and tablespoon of sugar to a bowl and whisk together. In a separate bowl, mix the flour and baking powder together, then tip into the buttermilk mixture and whisk together until smooth – the batter should be thick.

Place a frying pan over a medium–high heat and pour in the vegetable oil. Once the oil is hot, dip the reserved pieces of carrageen moss into the batter and then straight into the hot oil. Fry until they are golden and crispy. Remove to a bowl. Mix the remaining sugar and the cinnamon together, then toss the fritters in the cinnamon sugar.

Once the puddings have set, arrange the fritters on top and serve.

Orange Blossom Summer Sponge with Cream & Strawberries

MAKES 1 CAKE

This is such a showstopping cake! I just love seeing everyone's faces as I bring it to the table. The orange blossom is so soft and delicate, and adds a beautiful subtle flavour of orange to the cake. You can make the sponges a day ahead and then assemble with the cream and fruit before you serve. Gorgeous served as a dessert for a big supper or at an afternoon tea party.

6 eggs

330g caster sugar

330g self-raising flour, sifted

2 teaspoons baking powder, sifted

330g unsalted butter, softened, plus extra for greasing

2 tablespoons orange blossom water

1 teaspoon vanilla extract

FOR THE FILLING

500ml whipping cream

1 tablespoon orange blossom water

80g icing sugar, sifted, plus extra for dusting

600g jar strawberry jam

TO DECORATE

12 fresh strawberries

grated zest of 1 orange

Preheat the oven to 180°C/gas mark 4. Grease three 20cm sandwich cake tins and line the base of each tin with baking paper.

Crack the eggs into a large bowl, then add the caster sugar, flour, baking powder, butter, orange blossom water and vanilla extract. Beat all the ingredients together with an electric hand mixer or a wooden spoon until well combined.

Spoon the cake batter evenly between the prepared cake tins and tap the sides to release any air bubbles. Bake for 25 minutes or until the sponges are lightly golden brown.

Remove the cakes from the oven and leave to cool in the tins for about 15 minutes. Then remove them from the tins and transfer to a wire rack to cool completely.

While the cakes are cooling, prepare the filling. Lightly whip the cream, orange blossom water and icing sugar together in a bowl until light and fluffy.

To assemble, place one of the sponges, top facing downwards, on a cake plate or stand. Spread with some of the strawberry jam, followed by half the cream mixture. Repeat the process with another sponge, then add the third sponge, top facing upwards. Arrange the strawberries on top, then dust with icing sugar and sprinkle with the orange zest.

Sweet Geranium Cheesecake

MAKES 1 CHEESECAKE

The sweet geranium leaves give a beautiful delicate honey and lemon flavour to this cheesecake and the flowers look so pretty on top! I always have sweet geranium plants growing because they are great for using in baking, infusing creams and in syrups. If you don't have any sweet geranium leaves, you can use lemon verbena instead.

80g butter, plus extra for greasing

150g ginger biscuits

150g digestive biscuits

8 sweet geranium leaves, plus 10 for decoration, thoroughly washed

300ml double cream

350g cream cheese

150g caster sugar

First make the biscuit base. Lightly grease a 20cm springform cake tin or tart tin. Melt the butter in a small saucepan over a medium heat. Add all the biscuits to a food-processor and process to crumbs. Tip into a bowl, pour the melted butter over the biscuit crumbs and mix together well. Transfer the buttery crumbs to the greased tin, using the back of a spoon to spread and press them into an even, well-compacted base. Chill in the fridge for at least 30 minutes until firm and cold.

Add the eight sweet geranium leaves to a saucepan and stir in the cream. Place over a low heat, bring to a simmer and continue simmering for 10 minutes. Remove the pan from the heat and leave the cream to cool completely and infuse – about an hour.

Remove the geranium leaves from the cooled cream and then whip the cream.

Beat the cream cheese and sugar together in a large bowl until the sugar has dissolved and the mixture is smooth. Then fold in the sweet geranium-infused whipped cream.

Spread the cheesecake mixture on top of the biscuit base and arrange the extra sweet geranium leaves (or any decorative flowers) on top. Chill in the fridge for 2–3 hours until set before serving.

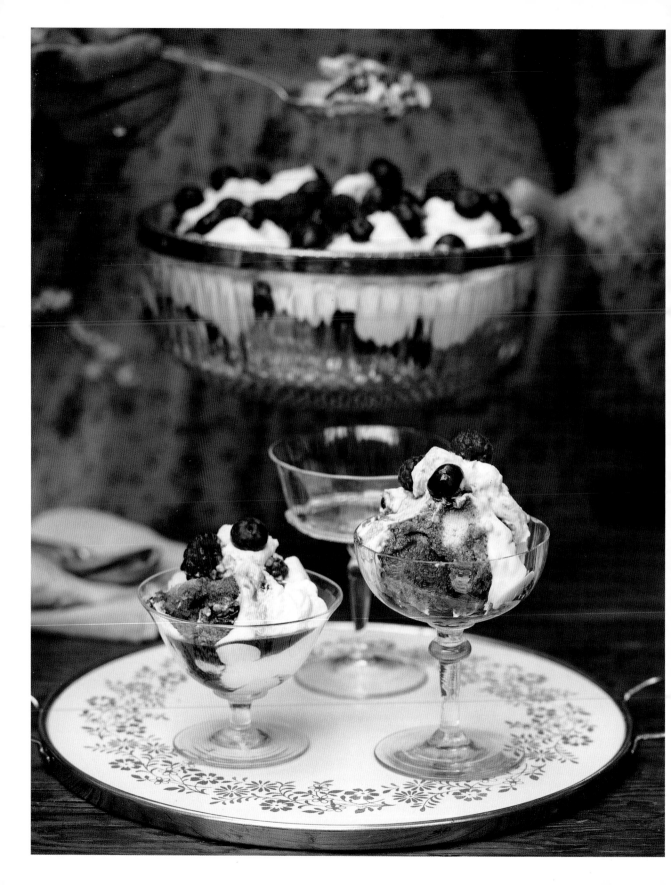

All-American Berry Trifle

SERVES 8

This trifle sings of summers in America – delicious pops of sweet summer berries, creamy mascarpone whipped with custard and infused with vanilla and set on Madeira or pound cake. On 4th July I top this trifle with flaming sparklers or mini American flags – it's my American hero dessert! You can make it up to a day ahead and it's great for entertaining a crowd. You can also serve it in smaller individual bowls but try to use glass so that you see the fabulous colours and layers.

450g fresh blueberries

375g fresh raspberries

75g caster sugar

3 tablespoons crème de cassis (optional)

300g Madeira cake, sliced

500ml ready-made cold custard

400g mascarpone cheese

1 tablespoon vanilla extract

300ml double cream, softly whipped

Place two-thirds of both berries and all the sugar in a saucepan and simmer over a low heat for 2 minutes. Pour in the crème de cassis, if using, then remove the pan from the heat and leave the mixture to cool.

Arrange a layer of the madeira cake slices in the base of a large trifle bowl, then spoon the berry mixture on top.

Add the custard, mascarpone and vanilla extract to a large bowl and whisk together until smooth, but ensure that the mixture doesn't become runny, as you want it to remain slightly thick. Spoon on top of the berry mixture, followed by the softly whipped cream.

Cover the bowl with clingfilm and chill in the fridge for a couple of hours. Just before serving, decorate the top of the trifle with the remaining berries.

Barbecued Peaches with Rosemary & Maple Butter

SERVES 6

The first time I had this dish was about ten years ago at a wedding in Tuscany, when they were served as the dessert. A barbecue was set up under a line of olive trees, and the juicy peaches were perfectly grilled, then passed along for a drizzle of rosemary maple butter and a dollop of mascarpone. They were sensational! I add a crumble of amaretti biscuit on top as it brings great texture.

6 ripe peaches

woody rosemary stalks, for skewers (or use wooden skewers)

240g butter

2 tablespoons chopped rosemary leaves

2 tablespoons maple syrup

150g mascarpone

6 amaretti biscuits, crumbled

Slice the ripe peaches in half through the middle and remove the stones. Thread the peach halves onto the rosemary stalks or wooden skewers.

Prepare a charcoal barbecue or heat a gas barbecue to a high heat, or place a griddle pan over a high heat. Grill the peaches, turning the skewers frequently, for about 10 minutes until they are soft.

While the peaches are grilling, place a saucepan over a low heat and add the butter, rosemary and maple syrup. Stir until the butter has melted, then leave to simmer for 5 minutes. Remove the pan from the heat.

Transfer the grilled peaches to dessert plates and drizzle the hot rosemary and maple butter over the peaches, followed by a dollop of mascarpone and a sprinkle of crumbled amaretti biscuits to serve.

Autumn Suppers

Menus

AUTUMN GATHERING

GRILLED MUSSELS WITH CHORIZO
& FLAT-LEAF PARSLEY BREADCRUMBS

SALMON FISHCAKES WITH
HORSERADISH CREAM

BANANA CAKE
WITH COCONUT FROSTING

FARMHOUSE CHEESE SUPPER

IRISH FARMHOUSE CHEESE SOUFFLÉ

COOLEA CHEESE POTATO DUMPLINGS
WITH SAGE BUTTER

ROASTED HAZELNUT
HOT CHOCOLATE PUDDINGS

FIRESIDE SUPPER

SALMON RILLETTES

WET PARMESAN POLENTA
WITH BLACK PUDDING

STICKY FIGGY CAKE

NEW YORK HARVEST

SMOKED HADDOCK & CORN CHOWDER

ROAST BUTTERNUT SQUASH, CASHEL
BLUE & SAFFRON PAPPARDELLE

BAKED APPLES WITH DATES & SPICES
SERVED WITH VANILLA CUSTARD

NORTHERN ITALIAN WILD
MUSHROOM SUPPER

WILD MUSHROOMS, LEMON & THYME
WITH RUNNY POACHED EGG

ROAST TARRAGON CHICKEN WITH
CHESTNUT MUSHROOM RISOTTO

VANILLA PANNA COTTA
WITH HONEYED FIGS

ONE-POT AUTUMN SUPPER

HONEY & THYME ROASTED FIGS, RICOTTA
& SOURDOUGH TOAST

CHOCOLATE BEEF CHILLI WITH
JALAPEÑO & CHEESE SCONES

ORANGE, PISTACHIO & YOGURT CAKE

SUNDAY ROAST

SPICED BUTTERNUT SQUASH
& COCONUT SOUP WITH PUMPKIN SEED
BREAD

ROAST PORK WITH APPLES
& BLACKBERRIES

BLACKBERRY BUTTER PASTRY PIE

Honey & Thyme Roasted Figs, Ricotta & Sourdough Toast

SERVES 6

Where I live in London, I have the most fantastic tropical garden with an enourmous fig tree, and during autumn I have an endless supply of delicious ripe figs. These figs simply roasted with thyme and honey are heavenly. You could leave out the sourdough toast if you wish and serve it as is.

12 fresh ripe figs

3 tablespoons clear Irish honey

2 tablespoons olive oil

1 tablespoon chopped thyme leaves

6 slices of sourdough bread

360g ricotta cheese

120g walnuts, chopped

sea salt and freshly ground black pepper

Preheat the oven to 180°C/gas mark 4.

Cut the figs into quarters and place on a baking tray.

Mix the honey, olive oil and thyme together in a small bowl. Drizzle half the mixture over the figs and toss to coat, or use a pastry brush to paint the figs with the mixture. Season with salt and pepper. Roast for 10 minutes.

While the figs are roasting, toast the sourdough bread, then cut the slices in half.

Arrange the sourdough toast, ricotta, walnuts and the roasted figs on a sharing platter or individual plates, and drizzle the remaining honey mixture over the figs and ricotta.

To eat, spread the ricotta onto the sourdough toast, followed by the honey and thyme figs, and add a sprinkle of chopped walnuts on top.

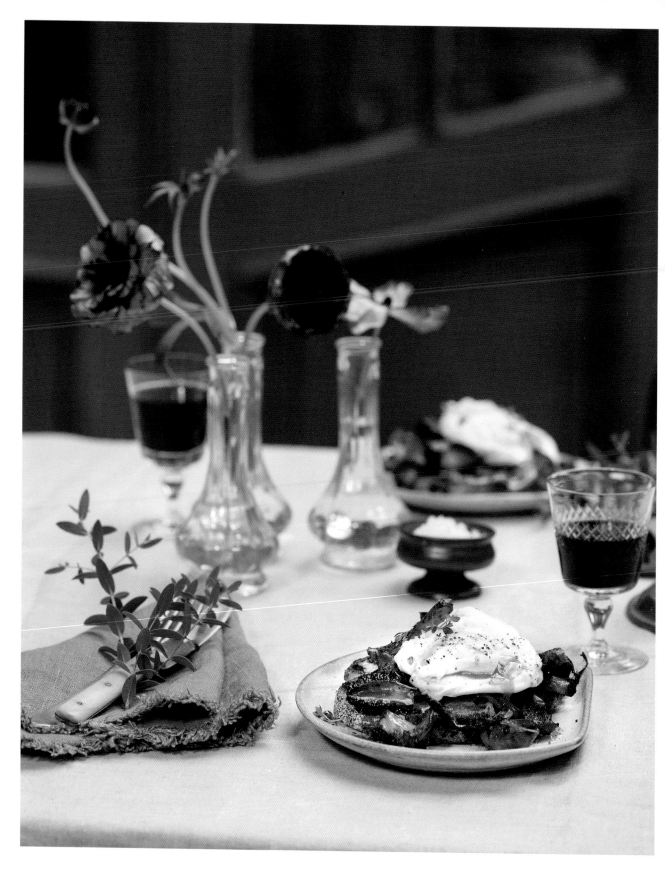

Wild Mushrooms, Lemon & Thyme with Runny Poached Egg

SERVES 2

This dish reminds me so much of autumns when I lived in Italy. When the wild mushrooms were in season, the market in the square in Turin would be filled with farmers selling amazing varieties from the Langhe region nearby. The soft-boiled egg oozing over the earthy mushrooms is utterly delicious! If you don't want to add the egg, then use shavings of Parmesan cheese instead.

200g wild mushrooms, such as chanterelles, morels or ceps

30g butter

2 tablespoons extra virgin olive oil

1 garlic clove, crushed

juice of 1 lemon

1 tablespoon finely chopped thyme leaves

2 eggs

sea salt and freshly ground black pepper

sourdough bread, to serve

Clean any grit off the mushrooms using a soft brush, then chop them up roughly.

Place a large frying pan over a medium heat and add the butter and olive oil. Once the butter has melted, toss in the mushrooms and crushed garlic, season with salt and pepper and add the lemon juice. Increase the heat and cook, tossing, for 3 minutes.

Sprinkle the thyme over the mushrooms and cook for a further minute.

While the mushrooms are cooking, poach the eggs in a saucepan of salted boiling water for just 4 minutes, then remove with a slotted spoon and drain on kitchen paper.

Divide the cooked mushrooms between two warmed plates and place a runny poached egg in the centre of each serving. Serve with fresh sourdough bread.

Irish Farmhouse Cheese Soufflé

These are my beautiful, light, fluffy cheese clouds! A dreamy starter or a main course for lunch. If you are frightened of the thought of making a soufflé, please don't be, as this recipe is so simple and completely foolproof. I also love making this with Gouda or Gruyère. It's best to make the mixture no more than 2 hours before cooking – as you might lose the lightness in the egg white.

20g fresh white breadcrumbs

40g butter, plus extra for greasing

40g plain flour

300ml milk

150g mature Irish Cheddar, grated

1 teaspoon Dijon mustard

4 large eggs, separated

Preheat the oven to 200°C/gas mark 6. Grease six small ramekins or other small ovenproof dishes and sprinkle with the breadcrumbs to coat.

Melt the butter in a saucepan over a medium heat. Stir in the flour and cook, continuing to stir, until a paste (roux) forms. Then gradually add the milk, whisking constantly, and cook until you have a smooth, thickened sauce.

Whisk in the grated Cheddar and mustard, followed by the egg yolks. Once the cheese has melted into the sauce and the consistency is smooth, remove the pan from the heat.

Put a kettle of water on to boil. Whisk the egg whites in a very clean and dry bowl until stiff. Stir a couple of spoonfuls into the cheese mixture to loosen it, then very slowly and gently fold in the remaining egg whites with a spatula. Divide the mixture between the prepared dishes.

Make a bain-marie by half-filling a roasting tin with boiling water from the kettle and place in the oven. Stand the dishes in the bain-marie and bake for 12 minutes until the soufflés are well risen and golden, then serve immediately.

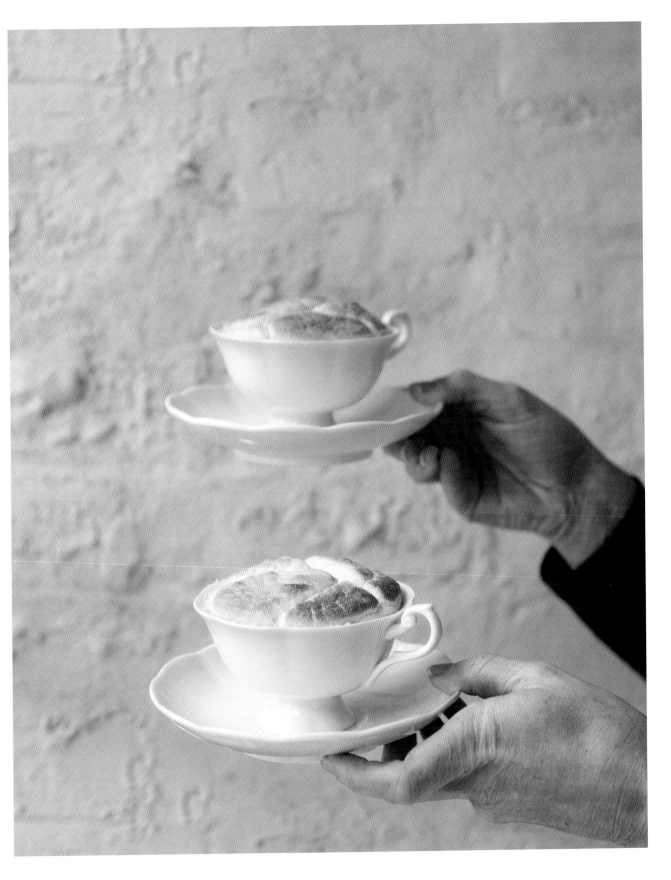

Smoked Haddock & Corn Chowder

SERVES 6

Where I was born in Cork, Ireland, is also home to some of the world's best fish smokers, such as Frank Hederman and Sally Barnes, to name just a couple. So I grew up eating lots of smoked fish and this smoked haddock chowder is one of my favourite ways to cook with it. The delicious smoky flavours infuse the creamy soup and the sweetness of the corn during autumn adds a ray of sunshine and sweetness. Make it in big batches so you can freeze ahead.

50g butter

300g potatoes, peeled and diced

1 onion, finely diced

1 leek, finely sliced

2 celery sticks, finely sliced

2 garlic cloves, crushed

100ml dry white wine

500ml hot fish stock

300ml milk

1 corn on the cob, husk and silky threads removed

1kg undyed smoked haddock fillet, skin removed and cut into small chunks

250ml single cream

2 tablespoons chopped dill

sea salt and freshly ground black pepper

Place a saucepan over a medium heat and add the butter. Once the butter has melted, add the potatoes, onion, leek, celery and garlic, stir well and cover the pan with a lid. Reduce the heat to low and leave the vegetables to sweat for 5 minutes, stirring once or twice.

Remove the pan from the heat and stir in the white wine. Return the pan to a medium heat and cook, uncovered, for 3–4 minutes.

Pour in the stock and milk and bring to the boil, then reduce the heat and simmer for 10 minutes.

Stand the corn cob upright on its base and run a sharp knife down its sides all round to remove the kernels, then add them to the saucepan. Gently stir in the haddock and simmer for 5 minutes.

Stir in the cream and dill and season to taste with salt and pepper. Cook for a further 5 minutes, then serve in warmed bowls alongside my Rosemary Clodagh Bread (page 203), if you wish.

Grilled Mussels with Chorizo & Flat-leaf Parsley Breadcrumbs

SERVES 6

Plump, sweet mussels with spicy, juicy chorizo, peppery flat-leaf parsley, aromatic garlic and crispy buttered breadcrumbs – sounds delicious, right? And it's so incredibly easy to make. This is the perfect easy starter to serve for supper or as a main dish at lunch. You can get the mussels prepared a day ahead and then just pop them under the grill before you serve. You can leave the chorizo out if you want a simpler garlic and herb flavour.

1kg live mussels, cleaned and beards removed (see page 85)

100ml water

50g butter, softened

3 garlic cloves, crushed

50g fresh cooking chorizo, skinned and diced

2 tablespoons chopped flat-leaf parsley

50g fresh white breadcrumbs

sea salt and freshly ground black pepper

Place the mussels in a saucepan with the water and bring to the boil over a high heat. Cover the pan with a lid and steam for 3 minutes or until all the mussels have opened (discard any that remain closed).

Drain the mussels, and when cool enough to handle, pull away and discard the top shells, leaving the mussels in the bottom shells. Place the mussels on a baking tray.

Preheat the grill to high. Add all the remaining ingredients to a bowl and season with salt and pepper, then mix well, using the back of a spoon to blend them together.

Spoon the breadcrumb mixture over the mussels using a teaspoon and flatten gently. Cook under the hot grill for 2–3 minutes until well browned. Serve.

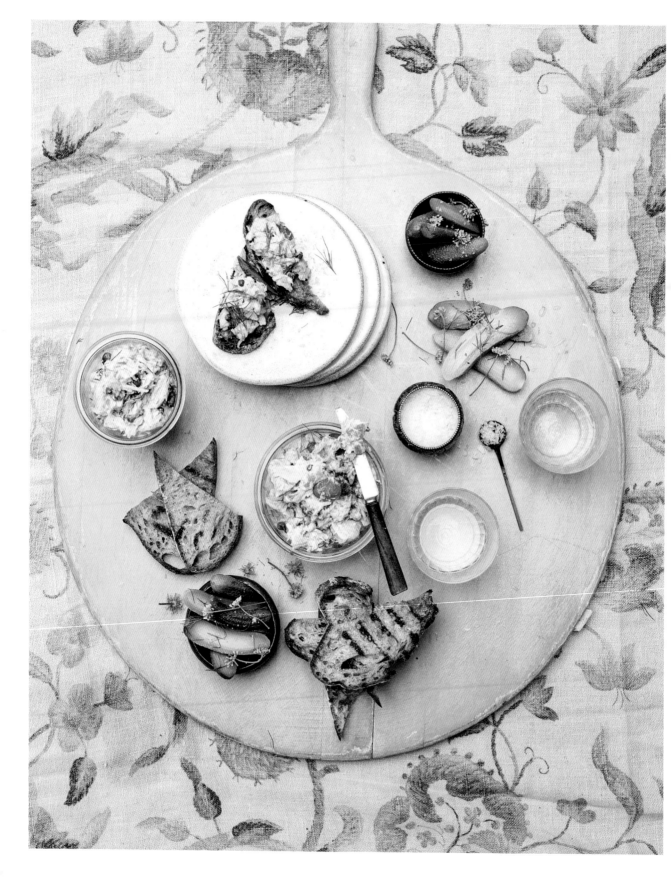

Salmon Rillettes

SERVES 4

I love serving these salmon rillettes as a sharing platter on a board with thinly sliced sourdough toast and pickles. You can get it made a couple of days before serving and it also works really well as picnic food or a packed lunch.

400ml dry white wine

2 shallots, finely chopped

400g skinless salmon fillet, chopped

100g smoked salmon, chopped

150ml crème fraîche

2 teaspoons finely chopped capers

1 tablespoon finely chopped dill

grated zest and juice of 1 lemon

sea salt and freshly ground black pepper

TO SERVE

thinly sliced sourdough bread, toasted

pickles

Place the white wine and shallots in a saucepan over a medium heat and bring to the boil, then reduce the heat to low. Add the fresh salmon and poach for 5 minutes. Using a slotted spoon, transfer the salmon to a plate lined with kitchen paper to drain. Strain the poaching liquid through a sieve, discarding the liquid, and transfer the shallots to a bowl. Add the poached salmon, cover the bowl with clingfilm and chill in the fridge until completely cooled.

Add the remaining ingredients to the poached salmon, season with salt and pepper and gently mix just to combine – the poached salmon will break up a little, but don't over-mix or the mixture will turn to a paste. Cover the bowl again and chill in the fridge.

Serve the salmon rillettes with thinly sliced, toasted sourdough bread and some pickles.

Spiced Butternut Squash & Coconut Soup with Pumpkin Seed Bread

SERVES 6

20g butter

1kg butternut squash, peeled, deseeded and cut into 2.5cm pieces

1 teaspoon ground cumin

1 teaspoon garam masala

2 garlic cloves, crushed

200g onions, chopped

700ml hot vegetable stock

300ml coconut milk

sea salt and freshly ground black pepper

FOR THE PUMPKIN SEED BREAD

200g plain flour, plus extra for dusting

1 teaspoon bicarbonate of soda

1 teaspoon fine sea salt

350g wholemeal flour

2 tablespoons pumpkin seeds

350ml milk, plus extra for brushing

250ml natural yogurt, plus extra for brushing

TO GARNISH

pumpkin seeds

raw coconut flakes

This soup is a ray of sunshine in a bowl during greyer days in autumn. The butternut squash is so sweet and creamy in the soup, and I love spicing and warming it up with cumin and garam masala. It does make a huge difference if you make your own vegetable stock.

Preheat the oven to 220°C/gas mark 7. Dust a baking tray with plain flour.

To make the bread, sift the plain flour, bicarbonate of soda and salt into a large bowl, then add the wholemeal flour. Using clean hands, mix the dry ingredients together with half the pumpkin seeds, then make a well in the centre.

Whisk the milk and yogurt together in a jug, then slowly pour into the well and use your free hand to mix the dry mixture into the wet mixture, trying to spread your fingers far apart so that your hand resembles a trough. Ensure that the resulting dough is entirely wet, with no dry patches remaining.

Pat your hands with plain flour and shape the dough into a round. Place on the floured baking tray. Dust a large knife with plain flour and use to cut the shape of a cross into the top of the dough, cutting about two-thirds of the way down through the dough.

Using a pastry brush, brush the dough with extra milk and yogurt mixed together. Sprinkle the remaining pumpkin seeds on top and press them gently into the dough. Bake for 25 minutes, then reduce the oven to 180°C/gas mark 4, and bake for a further 20 minutes. To test whether the loaf is cooked, tap the bottom with your knuckles – it should sound hollow. Transfer to a wire rack to cool.

To make the soup, place a heavy-based saucepan over a medium heat and melt the butter. Add the squash, spices, garlic and onions, and season with salt and pepper. Stir well, then reduce the heat to low, cover the pan with a lid and sweat for about 15 minutes, stirring every 5 minutes or so.

Stir in the hot stock and coconut milk and bring to the boil, then leave to cook, uncovered, for about 15 minutes until the squash is tender. Transfer the soup to a blender or food-processor and blend to a smooth consistency.

Return the soup to the saucepan and reheat. Serve in warmed bowls, topped with pumpkin seeds and coconut flakes, along with the pumpkin seed bread.

Roast Pork with Apples & Blackberries

SERVES 6

200g cooking apples, peeled, cored and diced

30 fresh blackberries

1 onion, finely diced

1 tablespoon finely chopped rosemary leaves

40g fresh white breadcrumbs

50g butter, melted

1.5kg boneless loin of pork

3 rosemary sprigs

sea salt and freshly ground black pepper

FOR THE APPLE CRISPS

2 cooking apples

ground cinnamon, for dusting

FOR THE APPLE & BLACKBERRY SAUCE

400g cooking apples, peeled, cored and roughly chopped

20 fresh blackberries

2 tablespoons caster sugar

50g butter

100ml water

1 rosemary sprig

Every autumn I go blackberry picking in the country. It's something I start to look forward to at the beginning of autumn and taking an afternoon to walk along the country roads, with a basket in hand foraging for the plumpest berries is heaven. Their juicy sweetness with the sour cooking apples, soaking into the pork while it roasts is incredible. The apple crisps are so simple to make and look fabulous dotted around the serving dish. I like to serve a creamy gratin dauphinoise with this dish or simple buttery mashed potatoes.

Preheat the oven to 220°C/gas mark 7.

Add the apples, blackberries, onion, chopped rosemary, breadcrumbs and melted butter to a large bowl, season with salt and pepper and mix well.

Butterfly the pork loin by making a slit down its length, cutting just deep enough so that you can open the loin up to lie flat like a book; don't cut all the way through.

Spoon the stuffing mixture onto the meat and spread it evenly, then close up the meat and secure it in its original shape by tying it together at intervals with kitchen string, tucking the rosemary sprigs under the string. Push in any stuffing that escapes from the ends.

Rub the joint all over with salt and pepper and place in a roasting tray. Roast for 25 minutes, then reduce the oven temperature to 180°C/gas mark 4, and roast for a further 1 hour 10 minutes (or 20 minutes per 450g).

While the pork is roasting, prepare the apple crisps. Core the apples and slice very thinly through the middle. Dust with cinnamon and lay on a baking sheet lined with baking paper.

Bake in the oven with the pork (at the lower temperature) for 45 minutes–1 hour, turning halfway through, until dried out and light golden, checking and removing any crisps that are ready as and when.

Meanwhile, make the apple and blackberry sauce. Place all the ingredients in a saucepan, cover the pan with a lid and cook gently, stirring every so often, for 15–20 minutes until the apples start to break down.

Once the pork is cooked, pour about 100ml of the cooking juices into the sauce and stir well.

Serve slices of pork with the hot apple and blackberry sauce and apple crisps.

Chocolate Beef Chilli with Jalapeño & Cheese Scones

50g salted butter

300g minced beef

1 small white onion or shallot, finely chopped

2.5cm piece of fresh ginger, peeled and grated

3 garlic cloves, crushed

1 teaspoon ground cumin

1 teaspoon ground cinnamon

3 small dried chillies, chopped

100g smoked bacon lardons

100g fully cured, ready-to-eat chorizo, diced

150ml red wine

400g can cherry tomatoes

300ml water

1 tablespoon brown sugar

2 teaspoons finely chopped fresh or dried oregano

2 bay leaves

1 tablespoon tomato ketchup

50g dark chocolate, grated

400g can red kidney beans, rinsed and drained

sea salt and freshly ground black pepper

FOR THE JALAPEÑO & CHEESE SCONES

225g plain flour, plus extra for dusting

1 tablespoon baking powder

pinch of fine sea salt

50g salted butter, chilled and cubed

125g Dubliner cheese, grated

2 fresh jalapeño chillies, finely chopped

125–150ml milk or buttermilk

SERVES 6

The chocolate in this utterly delicious chilli adds a fantastic silky texture as well as deep notes of cocoa. I always double the recipe when I am making it and freeze half. It's always better made the day ahead as the flavours improve over time.

Place a flameproof casserole dish over a medium heat and add half the butter. Once the butter has melted, add the minced beef and cook, stirring and breaking up with a wooden spoon, until browned. Transfer to a plate.

Add the remaining butter to the casserole dish, stir in the onion or shallot, ginger and garlic and cook for 2 minutes, then stir in the cumin, cinnamon and dried chillies and cook for a further minute. Add the bacon lardons and chorizo and cook, stirring, for about 3 minutes until lovely and crispy.

Return the beef to the pan and stir well. Pour in the red wine, stir and cook for 2 minutes. Then add the cherry tomatoes, water, brown sugar, oregano, bay leaves and ketchup, season with salt and pepper and stir well. Cover the pan with a lid and simmer over a low heat for 2 hours.

While the chilli is cooking, make the scones. Preheat the oven to 200°C/gas mark 6, and dust a baking tray with flour.

Sift the flour, baking powder and salt into a large bowl. Add the butter and rub in with your fingertips until the mixture resembles fine breadcrumbs.

Stir in half the grated cheese, followed by half the jalapeño chillies. Then gradually mix in enough milk or buttermilk with a fork to make a soft dough.

Roll out the dough on a floured work surface into a round about 1cm thick. Cut into six wedges, place on the floured baking tray and sprinkle the remaining cheese and jalapeños on top. Bake for 15 minutes until golden brown. Transfer the scones to a wire rack and leave to cool for 10 minutes.

Remove the lid of the casserole and stir in the dark chocolate and kidney beans, then simmer, uncovered, for a further 15 minutes. Serve with the jalapeño and cheese scones.

Salmon Fishcakes with Horseradish Cream

SERVES 4

I make these fishcakes when I am having a relaxed supper at home. They are so simple to cook, just combine all the ingredients together and shape into patties. You can make them a day ahead, and they also freeze very well. Fresh horseradish cream is a delicious peppery combo with the salmon and I also love serving the fishcakes with a chilli and tomato salsa or with a smoked paprika aioli (page 192).

FOR THE SALMON FISHCAKES

400g floury potatoes, boiled and mashed

400g skinless salmon fillet, poached and flaked

2 spring onions, finely chopped

2 teaspoons capers

1 tablespoon finely chopped dill

grated zest and juice of ½ lemon

50g butter

sea salt and freshly ground black pepper

FOR THE FRESH HORSERADISH CREAM

100ml crème fraîche

1 tablespoon peeled and grated fresh horseradish root

grated zest and juice of ½ lemon

2 teaspoons finely chopped flat-leaf parsley

1 lemon, cut into wedges, plus a bunch of watercress (optional), to serve

Preheat the oven to 180°C/gas mark 4.

Place all the ingredients for the fishcakes except the butter in a large bowl and season with salt and pepper. Mix until all the ingredients are well combined. Divide the fishcake mixture into four balls and shape each into a patty.

Place a frying pan over a medium heat and add the butter. Once the butter has melted, add the fishcakes and brown on both sides. Transfer the fishcakes to a baking tray and bake for 10 minutes.

While the fishcakes are baking, mix all the ingredients for the horseradish cream together in a small bowl, and season with salt and pepper.

To serve, place each fishcake on a warmed plate with a spoonful of the horseradish cream and a wedge of lemon, plus a handful of watercress, if you wish.

Roast Tarragon Chicken with Chestnut Mushroom Risotto

SERVES 4

This is my favourite way to cook and serve roast chicken during autumn. The tarragon adds a delicious sweet flavour, mixed with the spicy Dijon mustard and aromatic garlic. The risotto is creamy, so there is no need for a sauce. It's an ideal supper for a cosy evening at home.

100g butter, softened

2 garlic cloves, crushed

3 tablespoons finely chopped tarragon

2 teaspoons Dijon mustard

1 whole organic or free-range chicken, about 1.4kg

sea salt and freshly ground black pepper

FOR THE MUSHROOM RISOTTO

100g butter

2 shallots, very finely chopped

2 garlic cloves, crushed

300g Arborio (risotto) rice

100ml dry white wine

700ml hot chicken or vegetable stock

250g chestnut mushrooms, sliced

1 tablespoon finely chopped thyme leaves, plus extra to garnish

80g Parmesan cheese, grated

1 tablespoon mascarpone cheese

Preheat the oven to 200°C/gas mark 6.

Start by prepping the chicken. Add the softened butter, garlic, tarragon and mustard to a bowl, season with salt and pepper and mix well, using the back of a spoon to blend the ingredients together. Using clean hands, smear the butter mixture all over the chicken as well as underneath the skin.

Place the chicken in a roasting tray and roast for 1½ hours or until cooked through. To check if the chicken is cooked, insert a skewer into the thickest part of the thigh – the juices should run clear.

Meanwhile, to make the risotto, place a large saucepan over a medium heat and add half the butter. Once the butter has melted, stir in the shallots and garlic, then cover the pan with a lid, reduce the heat to low and leave to sweat for about 2 minutes until the shallots are softened but not browned.

Add the rice and stir to coat it with the butter, then cook, stirring, for a couple of minutes. Season with salt and pepper. Pour in the white wine, stir and cook for about 2 minutes until almost all of it has been absorbed.

Add the hot stock a ladleful at a time, cooking while stirring constantly after adding the stock until it has been absorbed before adding more. It should take 15–20 minutes for the rice to be cooked, but check by tasting as you go.

While the risotto is cooking, place a frying pan over a high heat, add the remaining butter and the mushrooms and cook, tossing, for 3 minutes. About 5 minutes before the rice is cooked, stir in the mushrooms and thyme, then stir in the Parmesan and mascarpone just before you serve the risotto.

Once the chicken is cooked, transfer it to a large serving platter and spoon the risotto all around it, then garnish with extra thyme.

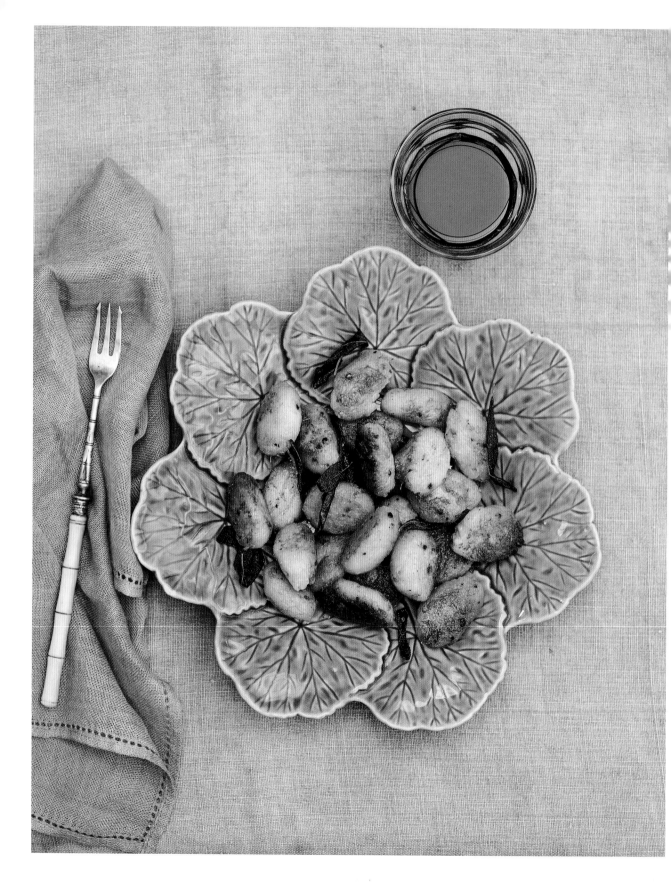

Coolea Cheese Potato Dumplings with Sage Butter

SERVES 4

Potato dumplings are a fantastic way to use up leftover mashed potato. You can also make these with sweet potatoes or add different cheeses to the mix. The dumplings have great texture – soft on the inside like little pillows and crispy on the outside. The sage butter is something I learned when living in Italy and is so delicious with these cheese dumplings or with egg tagliolini.

FOR THE POTATO DUMPLINGS

1kg Russet potatoes, unpeeled and washed

320g plain flour, plus extra for dusting

250g Coolea cheese, or use a mature Gruyère cheese, grated

1 egg yolk

sea salt and freshly ground black pepper

FOR THE SAGE BUTTER

100g salted butter

2 tablespoons finely chopped sage

For the potato dumplings, place the whole potatoes in a large saucepan, with the largest ones at the bottom, and fill the pan halfway with water. Cover the pan with a lid and place over a high heat. When the water begins to boil, drain off about half so that there is just enough left in the pan for the potatoes to steam. Leave to steam, covered, for 30–40 minutes, depending on the size of the potatoes, until soft.

Once the potatoes are cooked, hold them in a tea-towel while you peel them. Place them in a bowl and mash well or put through a potato ricer.

Mix the flour, grated cheese and egg yolk into the potatoes, and season with 2 teaspoons of salt and some pepper. Tip the dough onto a lightly floured work surface and knead lightly until well combined. Shape into three or four balls.

Dust the surface with more flour if necessary. Using your fingertips, roll each ball of dough into a sausage about 2cm in diameter. Cut into 2.5cm pieces, then roll each piece against the front tines of a fork to create ridges – this will help the sage butter cling to the dumplings once they are cooked.

Bring a large saucepan of salted water to the boil. Add the potato dumplings to the boiling water. When they rise to the surface, they are cooked, so quickly remove with a slotted spoon and drain well.

For the sage butter, place a frying pan over a medium heat and add the butter. Once the butter has melted, add the sage and cook until it is slightly crispy.

Tip the potato dumplings into the pan and mix them gently with the sage butter. Transfer to warmed serving plates and serve.

Roast Butternut Squash, Cashel Blue & Saffron Pappardelle

SERVES 2

This recipe is such a fast and easy dish to create and a great way to use up any leftover roast butternut squash. I crumble in Cashel Blue cheese, my favourite from Tipperary in Ireland, which is quite creamy and chalky in texture and has that unique ashy/smoky flavour. Next, a little crème fraîche to loosen it up and then comes the sunshine, as threads of saffron share their smokiness and enchanting colour with the sauce. The fresh pasta goes for a hot boiling sea salt swim for two minutes, then straight into the sunshine sauce, so that the pasta absorbs the flavours like bread soaking up gravy. Toss in the sweet butternut squash and sprinkle crunchy pumpkin seeds on top, then open a bottle of Barbera d'Asti, which has a lovely soft texture, with blackberry and Morello cherry flavours, and goes perfectly with this pasta. And ahh, we are in Rome with love from my London kitchen.

600g butternut squash

2 tablespoons olive oil

200ml crème fraîche

100g Cashel Blue cheese

½ teaspoon saffron threads

250g fresh pappardelle

20g pumpkin seeds

sea salt and freshly ground black pepper

Preheat the oven to 180°C/gas mark 4.

Halve the butternut squash and peel away the outer skin (use a good-quality vegetable peeler to make the task easier). Slice the squash into quarters and scoop out and discard the seeds, then cut the flesh into 1cm cubes.

Spread the squash out in a roasting tray, drizzle with the olive oil and season with salt and pepper. Roast for 35 minutes (you will notice the squash turning wrinkly), stirring every 10 minutes to ensure that it is well coated with the oil.

While the squash finishes roasting, place a frying pan over a low heat, add the crème fraîche and cheese and whisk together. Then whisk in the saffron and season with salt and pepper. Cook for a further 3 minutes until the sauce begins to thicken.

Bring a large saucepan of salted water to the boil over a high heat. Stir the pasta into the boiling water and cook for 3 minutes only – be careful, as it can very easily overcook.

Drain the pasta and return to the saucepan. Stir in the blue cheese and saffron sauce and the roasted squash and toss together really well, then transfer to a warmed serving dish. Sprinkle the pumpkin seeds on top before serving.

Wet Parmesan Polenta with Black Pudding

SERVES 4

I used to make wet polenta like this when I lived in Turin in Northern Italy because the winters were so cold and this is such an easy and warming dish. The black pudding adds great texture and flavours of sweetness as well as earthy spices. You will probably have some polenta left over, and if so, pour it into a dish, leave it to cool before you put it in the fridge where it will set, and you can then do a couple of things with it. You can slice it through the middle, add some fontina cheese and bake it in the oven or you can slice it into chips and fry them. It's also delicious served with roasted purple sprouting broccoli with Romesco sauce and crunchy seeds (see page 44).

150ml full-fat milk

600ml water

½ teaspoon sea salt

150g coarse polenta

1 tablespoon olive oil

280g black pudding

50g butter

100g Parmesan cheese, grated

1 teaspoon dried oregano

Pour the milk into a large saucepan along with the water and salt and bring to the boil.

Once the liquid has come to the boil, pour in the polenta in a thin, steady stream, whisking constantly. Cook, stirring, for 1–2 minutes until it thickens. Reduce the heat to low and cook, stirring well about every 5 minutes to prevent it sticking, for about 35–45 minutes until the polenta begins to come away from the sides of the pan.

While the polenta finishes cooking, place a frying pan over a medium heat and add the olive oil. Cut the black pudding into small pieces, add to the pan and cook until it becomes nice and crispy on the outside, stirring every couple of minutes so that it cooks evenly.

Once the polenta is ready, add the butter, Parmesan and oregano and stir until the butter and cheese have melted into the polenta.

Lastly, stir in the black pudding and then serve.

Baked Apples with Dates & Spices served with Vanilla Custard

SERVES 4

My dad used to love making spiced baked apples for us when we were growing up. They are so simple to prep, and look equally fabulous on the plate. The dates, cinnamon and nutmeg add delicious sweetness and spice to the apple, and there is nothing better to serve them with than a creamy custard. I do love to make my own custard, but if you are pressed for time, there are plenty of good ready-made versions that you can buy in the supermarkets. Get the apples prepped up a day ahead and then all that's left is to pop them in the oven before you sit down for the main course.

4 cooking apples

16 cloves

2 tablespoons clear Irish honey

100g dried pitted dates, finely chopped

2 teaspoons ground cinnamon

1 teaspoon freshly grated nutmeg

80g butter, melted

FOR THE CUSTARD

400ml milk

1 vanilla pod

3 egg yolks

30g caster sugar

1 teaspoon cornflour

Preheat the oven to 180°C/gas mark 4.

Remove the cores of the apples with an apple corer, then use a spoon to scoop out more of the apple to double the size of each cavity.

Stud around the middle of each apple with four cloves, then stand the apples in a shallow baking dish.

Place the honey, dates, cinnamon, nutmeg and melted butter in a small bowl and whisk together. Then pour the thick liquid into the cavity of each apple. Bake the apples for 30 minutes.

While the apples are baking, make the custard. Pour the milk into a saucepan and add the vanilla pod, then heat over a medium heat until just boiling.

Meanwhile, beat the egg yolks, sugar and cornflour together in a heatproof bowl until you have a smooth paste.

Gradually pour the hot milk over the egg yolk mixture, stirring constantly (remove the vanilla pod, then rinse, pat dry and reserve for use in another recipe). Pour the custard mixture into a clean saucepan and cook gently, stirring constantly, until it thickens.

Pour the hot custard over the baked apples just before serving.

Blackberry Butter Pastry Pie

SERVES 6

There is something so homely and warm about making a pie. It creates the most wonderful aroma in the kitchen and there is nothing like that familiar taste of butter pastry that I grew up on in Ireland. You can make it with lots of different fruits, such as apples, peaches, strawberries, raspberries and blueberries. Serve with a big dollop of softly whipped cream.

FOR THE PASTRY

225g butter, softened

55g caster sugar, plus extra for sprinkling

2 eggs, plus 1 egg, beaten, for glazing

grated zest of 1 lemon

340g plain flour, plus extra for dusting

FOR THE FILLING

300g fresh blackberries

140g granulated sugar

1 teaspoon ground cinnamon

grated zest of 1 lemon

whipped cream or vanilla ice cream, to serve

To make the pastry, place the butter and sugar in the bowl of a stand mixer or a large bowl and use the paddle attachment on the stand mixer or an electric hand mixer to beat on a high speed until pale and fluffy. Add the 2 eggs and lemon zest and beat for several minutes. Then add the flour and mix together on a low speed until a dough forms.

Turn the dough out onto a floured work surface and form into a ball, then wrap in clingfilm and chill in the fridge for at least an hour – this will give the pastry a crumblier texture once baked.

To make the pie, roll out two-thirds of the pastry (keep the remaining pastry wrapped in the fridge) on a lightly floured work surface to about 3mm thick and use to line a 23cm ovenproof flat plate, trimming the edges with a knife. Place in the fridge to chill while you wash and drain the blackberries.

Remove the pastry-lined plate from the fridge, then top with the blackberries in an even layer and sprinkle with the sugar, cinnamon and lemon zest.

Roll out the remaining pastry on a lightly floured work surface to about 3mm thick again and cut it into eight strips. Arrange and weave the pastry strips into a lattice pattern on top of the pie, then crimp all the way around the edge with your fingers and thumb to seal and neaten.

Brush the pastry all over with the beaten egg and sprinkle with caster sugar, then chill in the fridge for 30 minutes.

Meanwhile, preheat the oven to 180°C/gas mark 4.

Once chilled, bake the pie for about 45 minutes–1 hour until the blackberries are tender. Remove from the oven and then stand on a wire rack to cool for a while.

Serve the pie warm with whipped cream or vanilla ice cream.

Orange, Pistachio & Yogurt Cake

MAKES 1 CAKE

plain flour, for dusting

50g slightly stale white breadcrumbs

100g ground almonds

100g pistachio nuts, chopped

1 teaspoon baking powder

4 eggs

150g caster sugar

125ml sunflower oil, plus extra for oiling

200ml natural yogurt, plus extra to serve

grated zest of 1 orange

grated zest of 1 lemon

FOR THE CITRUS SYRUP

juice of 1 orange

juice of 1 lemon

100g granulated sugar

1 star anise

1 cinnamon stick

TO DECORATE

50g pistachio nuts, roughly chopped

grated zest of 1 orange

This is one of my favourite cakes at this time of the year. It's a much needed burst of sunshine and is deliciously light, and moist due to the natural yogurt. You can make a gluten-free version by simply using gluten-free breadcrumbs. You can substitute the pistachios with hazelnuts, but roast the hazelnuts before you add them to the cake as it really enhances their flavour. It will last for one week, but I am not sure you will have any left by then!

Preheat the oven to 190°C/gas mark 5. Oil a 20.5cm round cake tin, 5cm deep, then lightly dust with flour.

Add the breadcrumbs, ground almonds, pistachios and baking powder to a large bowl and mix together.

In a separate bowl, whisk the eggs and caster sugar together. Then gradually pour in the sunflower oil, whisking constantly, followed by the yogurt.

Add the wet mixture to the dry mixture and mix together well, then stir in the orange and lemon zest.

Pour the cake batter into the prepared tin and bake for 45 minutes–1 hour or until golden brown and a skewer inserted into the centre comes out clean.

While the cake finishes baking, make the citrus syrup. Place all the ingredients in a saucepan and bring gently to the boil, stirring until the sugar has dissolved completely. Simmer for 10 minutes or until thick.

When the cake is cooked, remove from the oven and leave to cool in the tin for 5 minutes before turning out onto a plate. While the cake is still warm, pierce it several times with a skewer, then spoon the hot syrup over the cake, allowing it to run into the holes. Leave the cake to cool completely, spooning any excess syrup back over the cake every now and then until it is all soaked up.

Sprinkle with the roughly chopped pistachios and orange zest to decorate, then serve with extra yogurt.

Vanilla Panna Cotta with Honeyed Figs

SERVES 4

There are so many different flavours and fruits that you can add to this panna cotta. The figs can be swapped for raspberries, blackberries, peaches or strawberries, or just serve it simply with no fruit at all. I have added lots of different extracts and waters too. Some of my favourites are rosewater, orange blossom water and lavender extract. I have also infused the panna cotta with different herbs, such as rosemary, lemon thyme, and lemon verbena – all are fabulous!

FOR THE PANNA COTTA

250ml double cream

I vanilla pod, slit lengthways

25g caster sugar

250ml milk

3 gelatine leaves

FOR THE FIGS

25g butter, melted

2 tablespoons clear Irish honey

I rosemary sprig, leaves picked and finely chopped

4 ripe figs, quartered

For the panna cotta, pour the cream into a saucepan, add the vanilla pod and sugar and bring to the boil, stirring until the sugar has dissolved. Reduce the heat and simmer for about 5 minutes until reduced by one-third. Remove the vanilla pod and when cool enough to handle, scrape the softened insides into the cream.

While the cream is reducing, pour the milk into a separate saucepan, add the gelatine leaves and leave to soak for about 15 minutes or until soft.

Remove the gelatine and set aside, then heat the milk until boiling, return the gelatine to the milk and stir until dissolved. Pour the milk and gelatine mixture through a sieve into the hot cream and then pour into four glasses. Leave to cool completely, cover and place in the fridge for an hour until set.

For the figs, preheat the oven to 180°C/gas mark 4.

Place the melted butter, honey and rosemary in a shallow baking dish and whisk together. Add the quartered figs and turn to coat with the mixture. Roast for about 15 minutes until the figs are tender and the cooking liquid is syrupy, brushing with the cooking liquid halfway through. Remove from the oven and leave to cool.

Remove the panna cotta from the fridge about 30 minutes before serving to warm up a little. Then spoon the honeyed figs on top of each panna cotta and serve.

Roasted Hazelnut Hot Chocolate Puddings

MAKES 6 INDIVIDUAL PUDDINGS

There's that moment when you spoon into the first bite of a hot chocolate pudding and wait for the delightful gooey chocolate interior to come running out into your spoon – heaven! The trick is not to overcook them as they really don't need more than 8 minutes to bake. Just ensure that your oven is properly preheated. You can make the mixture up a few hours ahead and store it in the fridge. The hazelnuts are so delicious crusted around the top and sides of the pudding – I also swap them with almonds, Brazil nuts or pistachios. If I have some nice berries, such as raspberries, blueberries or blackberries, I'll pop a few into the pudding mix too.

30g butter

100g blanched hazelnuts, very finely chopped

180g dark chocolate (70% cocoa solids), broken into chunks

4 eggs, separated

100g caster sugar

50g plain flour

Preheat the oven to 180°C/gas mark 4. Grease six ovenproof china cups or small ramekins with the butter, then sprinkle one-quarter of the finely chopped hazelnuts evenly around the inside of each, setting aside another quarter for topping the puddings.

Melt the chocolate in a heatproof bowl set over a saucepan of simmering water (don't let the base of the bowl touch the water).

While the chocolate is melting, in a separate bowl, whisk the egg yolks, sugar and the remaining 50g hazelnuts together.

Whisk the melted chocolate into the egg yolk mixture, then fold in the flour.

In another very clean and dry bowl, whisk the egg whites until stiff, then gently fold into the chocolate mixture.

Pour the pudding mixture into the prepared cups or ramekins and sprinkle the reserved hazelnuts on top. Stand on a baking sheet and bake in the oven for 9–10 minutes.

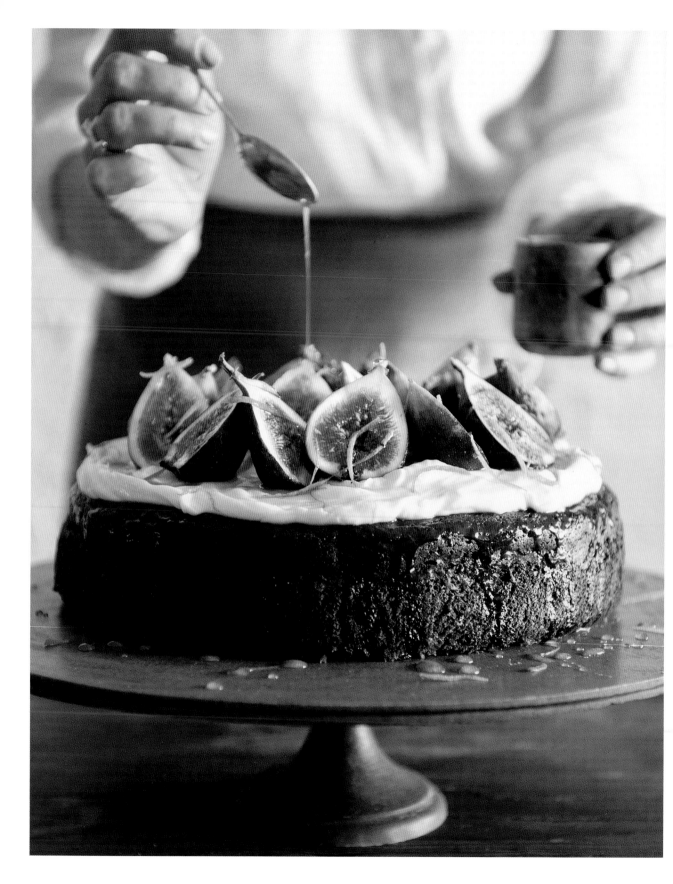

Sticky Figgy Cake

A true autumnal hero! I came up with this recipe as I had an abundance of figs from the tree in my garden, and I absolutely love a sticky toffee pudding – so this is a little similar in flavour but much lighter. Make sure you use ripe figs as they will add more flavour and you can leave out the frosting if you wish.

300g dried pitted dates

150g dried figs

900ml water

225g unsalted butter, softened, plus extra for greasing

350g light brown soft sugar

4 large eggs

2 teaspoons vanilla extract

300g self-raising flour

2 teaspoons bicarbonate of soda

150g fresh figs

FOR THE FROSTING

360g cream cheese, softened

200g icing sugar, sifted

TO DECORATE

12 fresh figs, halved

1 orange, for zesting

2 tablespoons clear Irish honey

Preheat the oven to 180°C/gas mark 4. Grease a 30cm springform cake tin.

Place the dates, dried figs and water in a saucepan over a medium heat and bring to the boil. Then reduce the heat and simmer for 30 minutes.

Remove the pan from the heat and leave the date and fig mixture to cool for 10 minutes, then transfer to a blender or food-processor and blend to a purée. Set aside.

Place the butter and sugar in the bowl of a stand mixer or a large bowl and use the paddle attachment on the stand mixer or an electric hand mixer to beat on a high speed until pale and fluffy. Add the eggs, one at a time, beating well after each addition, then beat in the vanilla extract. Fold in the flour and bicarbonate of soda, followed by the date and fig purée.

Pour the cake batter into the greased tin. Slice the fresh figs and place in a fan arrangement on top. Bake for 50–55 minutes or until golden brown and a skewer inserted into the centre comes out clean.

Remove the cake from the oven, then release the cake from the tin, transfer to a wire rack and leave to cool completely.

Meanwhile, make the frosting. Place the cream cheese and icing sugar in the bowl of the stand mixer or a large bowl and use the paddle attachment or an electric hand mixer to beat together on a high speed until well combined, light and fluffy.

Spread the frosting on top of the cooled cake. To decorate, arrange the halved figs on the frosting and zest the orange over the top. Lastly drizzle the honey over the cake.

Banana Cake with Coconut Frosting

MAKES 1 CAKE

I just love a good banana cake. Make sure you use very ripe bananas otherwise you don't get a good banana flavour. The frosting is light and fluffy, producing delicious exotic coconut flavours. You can use this frosting recipe for lots of different sponges and cakes and feel free to add different flavours like orange blossom water. Sprinkle raw coconut flakes on top as it adds great texture and looks so pretty... It is also, by the way, a fantastic way to use up bananas that have blackened.

110g unsalted butter softened, plus extra for greasing

150g light brown soft sugar

2 eggs

300g very ripe bananas, well mashed

4 tablespoons soured cream

½ teaspoon vanilla extract

190g plain flour, plus extra for dusting

1½ teaspoons baking powder

½ teaspoon bicarbonate of soda

2 teaspoons ground cinnamon

FOR THE COCONUT FROSTING

200g cream cheese, softened

40g unsalted butter, softened

50g icing sugar, sifted

3 tablespoons well-stirred cream of coconut

FOR THE FILLING

80g butter

2 bananas, sliced

30g raw coconut flakes, toasted, to decorate

Preheat the oven to 160°C/gas mark 3. Lightly grease a round 25cm cake tin and dust with flour.

Place the butter and brown sugar in the bowl of a stand mixer or a large bowl and use the paddle attachment on the stand mixer or an electric hand mixer to beat on a high speed until pale and fluffy. Add the eggs, one at a time, beating well after each addition, then add the mashed bananas, soured cream and vanilla extract and beat until well combined. Sift in the dry ingredients and mix together on a low speed.

Spread the cake batter into the prepared tin and bake for 45 minutes or until pale golden and a skewer inserted into the centre comes out clean.

Remove the cake from the oven and leave to cool in the tin for 10 minutes, then lift the cake out of the tin onto a wire rack to cool completely.

To make the frosting, place all the ingredients in the bowl of the stand mixer or a bowl and use the paddle attachment or electric hand mixer to beat together on a high speed until well combined, light and fluffy. This should take about 2 minutes.

For the filling, place a frying pan over a medium heat and add the butter. Once it has melted, add the banana slices and cook until golden brown and caramelised on both sides.

To assemble, slice the cooled cake in half horizontally. Spread half the frosting over the bottom half of the cake and arrange the caramelised bananas on top, then cover with the top half of the cake. Spread the remaining frosting on the top of the cake and sprinkle with the coconut flakes to decorate.

Winter Suppers

Menus

CHRISTMAS DAY

BRUSSELS SPROUT PETAL SALAD

ROSEMARY, CRANBERRY & CLEMENTINE
TURKEY WITH SWEET POTATO, BACON
& PECAN STUFFING

CHOCOLATE PECAN BROWNIE TRIFLE
WITH ORANGE BLOSSOM CREAM

COSY FAMILY SUPPER

KALE, BEAN & WINTER ROOTS SOUP

CORNED BEEF WITH SMASHED TURNIPS
& PARSLEY SAUCE

DATE & ALMOND BREAD & BUTTER
PUDDING

FONDUE NIGHT

CHICKEN LIVER PÂTÉ

WEEKEND FONDUE WITH BREAD
& PICKLES

TARTE TATIN WITH THYME

NEW YEAR'S EVE CELEBRATION

BAKED WHOLE VACHERIN MONT D'OR
WITH ROSEMARY CRISPBREADS

PORK TENDERLOIN FILLED WITH
BUTTERNUT SQUASH & HAZELNUTS
SERVED WITH MASHED CELERIAC

PLUM PUDDING ICE CREAM

ONE-POT WINTER SUPPER

GRILLED CAULIFLOWER WITH SUMAC
YOGURT, HAZELNUTS & POMEGRANATE

WINTER CHICKEN CASSEROLE

HOT CHOCOLATE AFFOGATO WITH
CANDIED ORANGE PEEL

WINTER GATHERING

CELERIAC SOUP WITH HAZELNUT & SAGE
PESTO

BEEF CASSEROLE WITH HERBY
POTATO DUMPLINGS

CASHEL BLUE OAT CHEESECAKE WITH
IRISH HONEY

WINTER SEAFOOD SUPPER

CRAB, BLOOD ORANGE & FENNEL SALAD

FISH PIE WITH DUBLINER CHEESE RÖSTI
TOPPING

STAR ANISE & ORANGE RICE PUDDING

Brussels Sprout Petal Salad

SERVES 4

This is such a refreshing way to serve Brussels sprouts, which are so delicious in a salad. It does take a bit of time to peel off the petals, but you can get this done a day ahead and store them in a bowl covered with damp kitchen paper in the fridge. I swap out the kale sometimes with green salad leaves like Cos, rocket and watercress. The walnuts are delicious in this salad as they go so well with blue cheese, but you could use hazelnuts, almonds or pine nuts instead. This starter is so light and festive and a gorgeous way to start your Christmas or any winter supper. It also works perfectly as a lunch dish.

1 tablespoon olive oil

200g diced pancetta

300g Brussels sprouts

200g kale

100g walnuts, toasted and chopped

80g dried cranberries

100g blue cheese

FOR THE DRESSING

1 teaspoon Dijon mustard

100ml extra virgin olive oil

grated zest and juice of 1 lemon

sea salt and freshly ground black pepper

Place a frying pan over a medium heat and add the olive oil. Once the oil has warmed, add the pancetta to the pan, increase the heat to high and cook, tossing, for 2–3 minutes until the pancetta is crispy. Remove the pan from the heat and set aside.

Place a saucepan of water over a high heat and bring to the boil.

Meanwhile, prepare the Brussels sprouts by removing and discarding the outer petals, then peel away all the remaining petals and place them in a bowl. Slice the kale into thin strips.

Add the kale strips to the boiling water for 30 seconds, then drain and pat dry with kitchen paper. Place in the bowl with the Brussels sprout petals.

To make the dressing, place the mustard, extra virgin olive oil and lemon zest and juice in a small bowl. Season with salt and pepper and whisk together.

Sprinkle the toasted walnuts, dried cranberries and crispy pancetta into the bowl with the Brussels sprout petals and kale, then crumble the blue cheese on top. Pour the dressing over the salad and toss together well.

Divide between four serving plates or serve in a large bowl.

Baked Whole Vacherin Mont d'Or with Rosemary Crispbreads

SERVES 4

This is my go-to starter in the winter when I am a bit pushed for time but want something utterly delicious so my guests don't feel like I'm cheating! The first time I tasted this recipe was in my friend Giana Ferguson's house in Gubbeen Farm, West Cork – she makes the famed Gubbeen cheese. She served this to me in her cosy farmhouse kitchen using her semi-soft Gubbeen cheese – I can still remember the sensation of scooping the crunchy, warm bread into the gooey aromatic cheese and that first mouthful of silky-smooth cheese infused with rosemary and garlic!

FOR THE CRISPBREADS

100ml warm water

½ teaspoon fast-action dried yeast

210g plain flour, plus extra for dusting

2 tablespoons olive oil, plus extra for oiling and brushing

3 rosemary sprigs, leaves picked and finely chopped, plus extra sprigs, to decorate (optional)

sea salt and freshly ground black pepper

FOR THE BAKED CHEESE

1 whole Vacherin Mont d'Or

2 garlic cloves, crushed

1 tablespoon finely chopped rosemary leaves

50ml dry white wine

To make the crispbreads, pour the water into a bowl, sprinkle in the yeast and whisk together well. Leave for 5 minutes until the mixture starts to foam.

Sift the flour into a large bowl and make a well in the centre. Pour the yeast mixture into the well and add the olive oil and a sprinkle of salt. Stir together until a dough forms – it should be moist but not sticky.

Tip the dough onto a floured work surface and knead for 10 minutes. Transfer to an oiled bowl, cover with a clean tea-towel or clingfilm and place in a warm, dry spot, such as an airing cupboard, for an hour.

Preheat the oven to 180°C/gas mark 4. Line a large baking sheet with greaseproof paper (or use two baking sheets). Divide the dough into eight pieces and roll out each piece on a lightly floured work surface into a rectangle measuring about 24 x 10cm. Transfer to the lined baking sheet. Brush with olive oil and sprinkle with the chopped rosemary and some salt.

Bake for 15 minutes or until crisp and golden. Remove from the oven and leave to cool on wire racks.

To prepare the baked cheese, remove the lid from the cheese box. Make several slits in the top of the cheese with a sharp knife and sprinkle over the crushed garlic, chopped rosemary and white wine. Season with salt and pepper. Place the lid back on the cheese box, sit the box on a baking tray and bake for 15 minutes until melted.

To serve, remove the lid from the cheese box and place the box on a wooden serving board, then arrange the crispbreads around the cheese and scatter over some sprigs of rosemary for decoration, if you wish.

Grilled Cauliflower with Sumac Yogurt, Hazelnuts & Pomegranate

SERVES 4

This starter is so beautiful to look at – like a flower on a plate with drizzles of sunshine sprinkled on top. It's a very healthy start to your supper and a great vegetarian option as a main course. If you want to make it vegan, then just use coconut yogurt instead of natural yogurt, which is equally delicious. You can swap out the cauliflower for grilled aubergines or courgettes if you wish. The dressing can be made a day ahead and refrigerated.

1 cauliflower

100ml natural yogurt

1 tablespoon extra virgin olive oil

juice of ½ lemon

2 teaspoons sumac

80g blanched hazelnuts

seeds of ½ pomegranate (see page 70)

sea salt and freshly ground black pepper

Preheat the grill to high. Remove the green leaves from the cauliflower, then slice the cauliflower vertically into slices 2.5cm thick. Place on a baking tray and cook under the grill for 5 minutes on each side.

While the cauliflower is grilling, make the dressing. Place the yogurt, extra virgin olive oil, lemon juice and sumac in a bowl. Season with salt and pepper and whisk together well.

Place a frying pan over a high heat, add the hazelnuts and lightly toast, shaking the pan frequently to toast the nuts evenly, for 2 minutes. Remove from the pan and leave until cool enough to handle, then roughly chop.

Place the grilled cauliflower on a sharing platter or divide between four individual plates. Drizzle the sumac yogurt dressing on top, followed by a sprinkle of the chopped hazelnuts and pomegranate seeds.

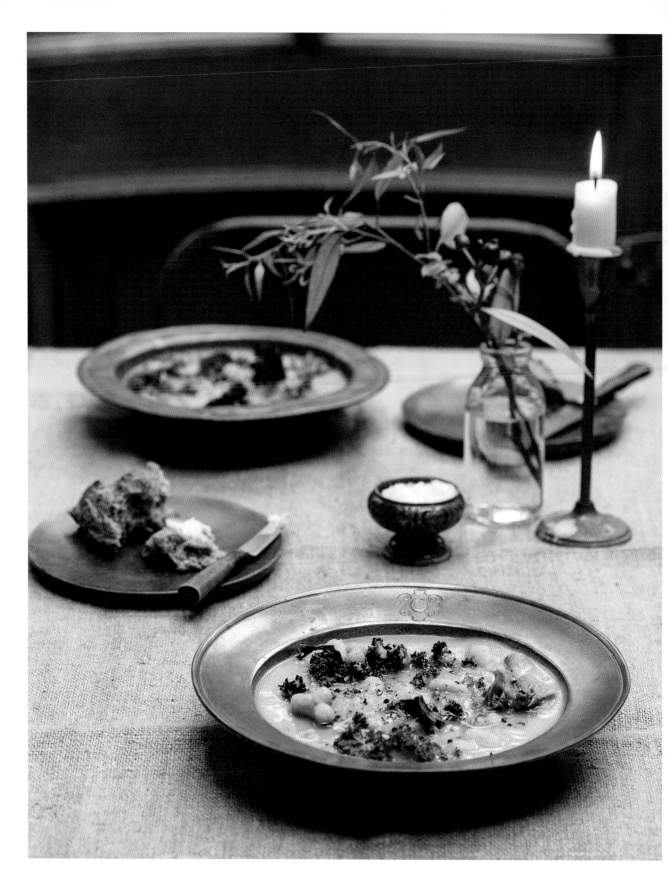

Kale, Bean & Winter Roots Soup

SERVES 6

My gorgeous friend, florist Nikki Tibbles, has the most beautiful house in the country and I have been lucky enough to spend many weekends there, foraging, cooking and sharing suppers together. She makes a big batch of soup every weekend with whatever seasonal vegetables she has and packs it up for her busy week back in London. This recipe is inspired by one of her soups. It feels so nourishing during the winter months when we need lots of goodness to protect ourselves from colds. Plus it's absolutely delicious and full of colour. Make it in big batches so that you can freeze and use throughout the week.

3 tablespoons olive oil

3 carrots, peeled and cubed

3 parsnips, peeled and cubed

2 celery sticks, cubed

1 onion, diced

2 teaspoons finely chopped rosemary leaves

3 garlic cloves, crushed

1 litre hot chicken or vegetable stock

250g cavolo nero (black or Tuscan kale), chopped

2 x 400g cans cannellini beans, rinsed and drained

sea salt and freshly ground black pepper

TO SERVE

50g Parmesan cheese, shaved

1 tablespoon finely chopped rosemary leaves

Place a large, heavy-based saucepan or flameproof casserole dish over a low heat and pour in the olive oil, then add the carrots, parsnips, celery, onion, rosemary and garlic. Season with salt and pepper and stir well. Cover the pan with a lid and leave the vegetables to sweat for 15 minutes, stirring every 5 minutes or so.

Stir in the hot stock and bring to the boil, then leave to cook for 10–15 minutes or until all the vegetables are tender.

Transfer the soup to a blender or food-processor, or use a hand blender, and blend to a smooth consistency.

Return the soup to the saucepan or casserole dish (if necessary). Stir in the cavolo nero and cannellini beans and cook for 3–4 minutes until the kale has wilted and the beans have heated through. Season to taste.

Divide the soup between warmed bowls and sprinkle with the Parmesan cheese shavings and rosemary to serve.

Chicken Liver Pâté

SERVES 10

I started making this pâté about 16 years ago when I had a few stalls at various farmers' markets in Ireland. It is one of my classic recipes that I love to cook about once a month. I store the leftovers in a Kilner jar so I can dip in and out of it for snacks and lunch. I like to serve it with cucumber pickle and my Spicy Apple Chutney (see page 201) and with thinly sliced sourdough toast. I have so many variations to this recipe but my favourite is adding about 100g smoky pancetta and fresh rosemary instead of the thyme. It will store well in the fridge, so you can make this a couple of days ahead.

450g butter, softened

675g chicken livers, cleaned

3 tablespoons brandy

3 garlic cloves, crushed

1 tablespoon thyme leaves

sea salt and freshly ground black pepper

TO SERVE

Spicy Apple Chutney (page 201)

thinly sliced sourdough

Place a frying pan over a medium heat and add a knob of the butter. Once the butter has melted, add the chicken livers and cook for about 15 minutes or until thoroughly cooked with no trace of red remaining, stirring occasionally and breaking up the livers with a wooden spoon. Transfer the cooked livers to a blender or food-processor.

Add the brandy, garlic and thyme to the frying pan and deglaze the pan by scraping up all the tiny pieces of meat and juices from the livers with a whisk – the base of the pan is where the real flavour is! Add the brandy mixture to the blender or food-processor and process until well blended. Leave to cool.

Gradually add the remaining butter to the cooled chicken liver mixture and blend until all the butter has been incorporated and you have a silky-smooth consistency.

Transfer the chicken liver pâté to a large dish, cover with clingfilm and chill in the fridge for at least 3 hours until set.

Serve the pâté with my apple chutney and rosemary bread (page 203).

Crab, Blood Orange & Fennel Salad

SERVES 2

This salad is like a ray of sun in the middle of winter and is perfect as a starter or a main course for lunch. I absolutely love blood oranges, buy the small ones as they are much sweeter and once you slice into them the vibrant colours will make you instantly smile. The vibrant zestiness of the blood orange enhances the crab, and the fennel adds a gentle fragrance. The added crumble of hazelnuts on top brings great texture but you could also use almonds instead.

½ fennel bulb, halved and very thinly sliced

1 tablespoon extra virgin olive oil

200g cooked white crab meat

1 tablespoon finely chopped dill

2 teaspoons crème fraîche

2 small blood oranges (or 1 large blood orange)

50g blanched hazelnuts, toasted and chopped (see page 148)

sea salt and freshly ground black pepper

Add the sliced fennel to a bowl and pour over the extra virgin olive oil to coat. Add the crab meat, dill and crème fraîche, season with salt and pepper and toss together.

Thinly slice the whole blood oranges – I leave the skin on when I'm slicing them, as you get a much cleaner cut, then I cut the skin off the slices with a sharp knife.

Divide the crab salad between two plates and arrange the sliced blood oranges on top of the salad, followed by a sprinkle of the chopped toasted hazelnuts. Serve.

Celeriac Soup with Hazelnut & Sage Pesto

SERVES 6

This is my favourite soup to make during the winter months. The flavour of the celeriac is celery-like with nutty undertones, and the consistency of the soup is so creamy. The pesto also adds delicious crunchy texture and earthy flavour. You can make it a few days ahead as it freezes really well, so double the recipe when you are making it so you have a batch for a rainy day! I sometimes add a crumble of crispy, smoky pancetta on top with the pesto.

50g butter

1 celeriac, peeled and chopped

1 celery stick, chopped

1 onion, chopped

75g blanched hazelnuts

1 litre hot vegetable stock

100ml crème fraîche

sea salt and freshly ground black pepper

FOR THE HAZELNUT & SAGE PESTO

75g blanched hazelnuts

2 tablespoons finely chopped sage

2 tablespoons extra virgin olive oil

Place a heavy-based saucepan over a medium heat and add the butter. Once the butter has melted, add the celeriac, celery, onion and whole hazelnuts, and season with salt and pepper. Stir well, then reduce the heat to low, cover the pan with foil or your butter wrapper and pop the lid on. Leave the vegetables to sweat for 15 minutes.

Next make the hazelnut and sage pesto. Place a frying pan over a high heat, add the hazelnuts and toast, shaking the pan frequently to toast the nuts evenly, for 3 minutes – this will release all the oils and the flavour.

Add the chopped sage to the extra virgin olive oil in a small bowl.

Tip the toasted hazelnuts onto one half of a clean tea-towel, then fold over the other half of the tea-towel to cover and bash the nuts with a rolling pin until crushed. Add the crushed nuts to the olive oil and sage, mix together well and set aside.

Add the hot stock to the vegetables and bring to the boil, then leave to cook, uncovered, for about 15 minutes until the vegetables are tender.

Transfer the soup to a blender or food-processor, or use a hand blender, and blend to a smooth consistency.

Return the soup to the saucepan (if necessary). Stir in the crème fraîche and place over a medium heat for just 2 minutes to warm through.

Serve the soup in warmed bowls with the hazelnut and sage pesto drizzled on top.

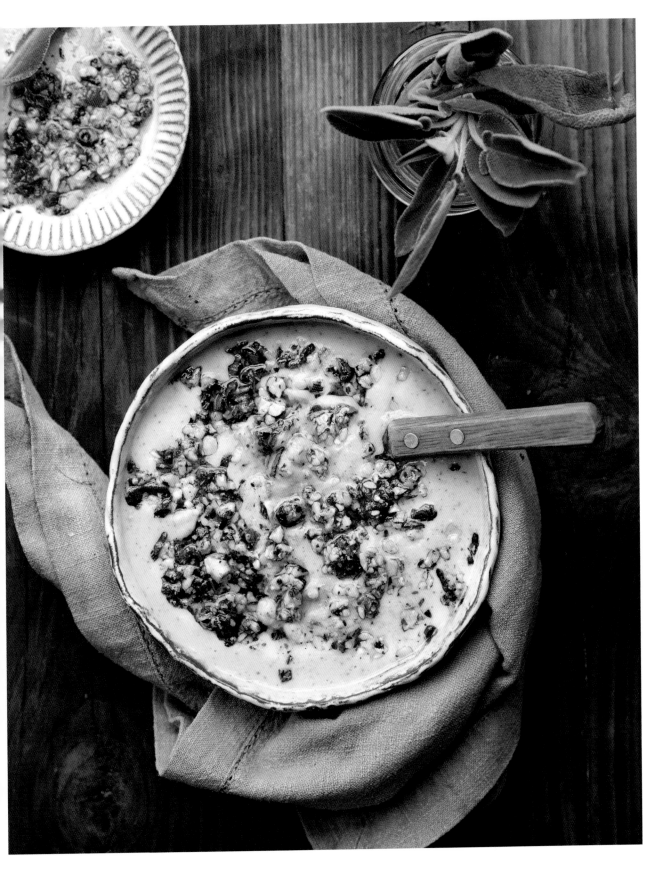

Winter Chicken Casserole

SERVES 4

80g butter

1 whole organic or free-range chicken, about 1.4kg, cut into 8 pieces

8 shallots, peeled and left whole

4 carrots, peeled and chopped into 5cm pieces

2 parsnips, peeled and chopped into 5cm pieces

4 garlic cloves, peeled and left whole

16 baby potatoes, washed

250ml dry white wine (optional)

1 litre hot chicken stock

grated zest and juice of 1 lemon, leftover lemon reserved

1 tablespoon clear Irish honey

1 tablespoon Dijon mustard

2 flat-leaf parsley sprigs, chopped

4 thyme sprigs

1 sage sprig

2 bay leaves

sea salt and freshly ground black pepper

green leaf salad, to serve

I love to get a big pot of this hearty chicken casserole on in the afternoon or the evening before and then reheat it before serving. The flavours enhance so much if you make it a day ahead, but either way it's a lovely warming supper dish to serve during the winter. I sometimes add leeks or cherry tomatoes on their vines if I have them. You don't have to use a whole chicken and I often use chicken thighs or breasts with the bones in them. I say to use chicken stock in the recipe, but I often have a pot of vegetable broth brewing which works just as well. Any leftover chicken is delicious in a chicken salad the next day.

Preheat the oven to 180°C/gas mark 4.

Place a flameproof casserole dish over a medium heat and add half the butter. Once the butter has melted, add the chicken pieces, in batches, skin-side down, and sear over a medium-high heat until lightly browned, then season with salt and pepper. Remove from the casserole dish and set aside.

Add the remaining butter to the casserole dish, stir in the shallots, carrots, parsnips and garlic and cook until lightly browned.

Return the seared chicken to the casserole dish and stir in the baby potatoes. Pour in the white wine and simmer for 5 minutes to allow the alcohol to evaporate – adding the wine is optional, but it does give a beautiful flavour.

Whisk the stock, lemon zest and juice, honey and mustard together, then pour into the casserole dish. Slice up the leftover lemon and add to the dish. Lastly, stir in the herbs.

Cover the casserole dish with the lid, transfer to the preheated oven and cook for 1½ hours.

I like to present this casserole in its dish in the centre of the table, and serve my family and friends at the table to create a relaxed atmosphere. Serve with a fresh green leaf salad.

Beef Casserole with Herby Potato Dumplings

SERVES 6

650g boneless stewing beef, cut into 5cm chunks

20g plain flour

80g butter

8 shallots, peeled and left whole

200g diced pancetta

2 garlic cloves, crushed

200g chestnut mushrooms, quartered

100g whole peeled chestnuts, roughly chopped

400ml Irish stout

200ml hot beef stock

1 teaspoon finely chopped thyme leaves

2 tablespoons grated dark chocolate or nibs

sea salt and freshly ground black pepper

FOR THE HERBY POTATO DUMPLINGS

1kg potatoes, peeled

80g butter

2 tablespoons finely chopped flat-leaf parsley

1 tablespoon finely chopped sage

1 tablespoon finely chopped thyme leaves

200g plain flour, plus extra for dusting

FOR THE ROUX

50g butter

50g plain flour

The longer you can leave the casserole to cook over a low heat the better, as the beef will keep tenderising. I like to serve slices of roasted butternut squash tossed in olive oil, ground cumin and garlic as a side dish to this casserole. By the way, the chocolate in this recipe is not a mistake. The French have being doing it for years and it adds a fabulous rich flavour and velvety texture – you will love it.

Preheat the oven to 140°C/gas mark 1. Place the beef in a large bowl, sprinkle with the flour and season with salt and pepper. Toss to coat.

Place a flameproof casserole dish over a medium heat and melt half the butter. Add all the beef and cook, stirring occasionally, for about 5 minutes until browned. Transfer the beef to a bowl.

Add the shallots and pancetta to the casserole dish and cook for 5 minutes. Increase the heat to get the pancetta really crispy and the shallots golden brown. Transfer the shallots and pancetta to the same bowl as the beef. Add the remaining butter to the casserole dish, then stir in the garlic, mushrooms and chestnuts and cook for 3 minutes.

Return all the browned ingredients to the casserole dish, pour in the stout and stock and stir in the thyme and chocolate. Bring to the boil, then cover the casserole dish with the lid, transfer to the oven and cook for 1 hour.

Meanwhile, make the dumplings. Place the potatoes in a saucepan and fill halfway with water. Cover with a lid and bring to the boil, then reduce the heat and simmer for 30–35 minutes or until the potatoes are completely cooked.

Drain the potatoes and tip into a bowl. Season, add the butter and finely chopped herbs and mash well. Add the flour and stir to combine. Dust your hands with flour, then shape the potato and herb mixture into dumplings slightly smaller in size than a tennis ball. You should be able to make six.

Before you add the dumplings to the stew, make the roux. Once the casserole has cooked for an hour, remove from the oven. Melt the butter in a small saucepan over a medium heat, stir in the flour, then gradually strain all the liquid from the casserole into the roux, whisking constantly, and cook until the sauce is thick and smooth. Pour the sauce back into the casserole.

Arrange the herby potato dumplings on top of the stew so that it is completely covered, return to the oven, without the lid, and bake for 35 minutes. Serve.

Corned Beef with Smashed Turnips & Parsley Sauce

SERVES 6

On cold winter evenings in London when I miss home, I make my way to the local butcher and get myself a salt-cured silverside of beef. Once I am back in my kitchen I get the beef cooking and turn it into what we call corned beef, very similar to the Jewish salted beef. Served with buttery golden turnips and creamy peppery parsley sauce, this is my Irish comfort food that makes me so happy.

1kg salt-cured silverside beef joint

2 bay leaves

1 onion, chopped

sea salt and freshly ground black pepper

FOR THE TURNIPS

400g turnips, peeled and chopped

50g butter

FOR THE PARSLEY SAUCE

25g butter

1 onion, finely diced

2 tablespoons plain flour

200ml milk

2 tablespoons finely chopped curly parsley

1 teaspoon English mustard

pinch of freshly grated nutmeg

Place the beef, bay leaves and onion in a large saucepan, cover with water and bring to the boil over a high heat. Reduce to a simmer and skim off the foam that accumulates on the surface of the water. Cover the pan with a lid and simmer for about $2\frac{1}{2}$ hours or until the beef is tender.

Remove the beef from its cooking liquid, wrap in foil and set aside. Reserve about 400ml of the cooking liquid.

For the turnips, place them in a saucepan with half the reserved beef cooking liquid. Bring to the boil, then reduce the heat and simmer for 20 minutes or until tender.

Drain the turnips and return to the pan. Add the butter and season with salt and pepper. Smash the turnips roughly using a potato masher.

To make the parsley sauce, melt the butter in a saucepan over a medium heat. Stir in the onion and cook for 1 minute, then stir in the flour and cook, stirring, for about a further minute. Add the remaining reserved beef cooking liquid, the milk, parsley, mustard and nutmeg, and season with salt and pepper. Continue to whisk until you have a smooth consistency. Cook for another 3 minutes, whisking constantly, until the sauce thickens.

To serve, slice the beef against the grain onto a warmed platter and spoon the smashed turnips alongside. Pour the parsley sauce into a warmed jug and then over the meat when you are ready to serve.

Rosemary, Cranberry & Clementine Turkey with Sweet Potato, Bacon & Pecan Stuffing

SERVES 8

1 organic or free-range turkey, 4–4.5kg

Sweet Potato, Bacon & Pecan Stuffing (see page 165)

sea salt and freshly ground black pepper

FOR THE FLAVOURED BUTTER

150g salted butter, softened

75g dried cranberries, very finely chopped

4 rosemary sprigs, leaves picked and finely chopped

grated zest of 1 clementine, then fruit peeled, segmented and chopped

FOR THE ROASTING TRAY

4 shallots, peeled and halved

3 carrots, peeled and cut into 7.5cm pieces

1 garlic bulb, halved through the middle

4 small bunches of thyme

4 small bunches of sage

2 clementines, halved

The clementines and cranberries are so festive and together with the fresh rosemary they pack lots of delicious flavours into the turkey. I love dressing the turkey platter with slices of clementines and sprigs of fresh rosemary. Do ensure you take the turkey out of the fridge at least an hour before you put it in the oven as it will give you a more tender result. You can dress the turkey in the flavoured butter a day ahead and use it for a turkey crown or leg also.

If you are using a frozen turkey, it is best to defrost the bird in the fridge. It will need about 24 hours to defrost for every 2kg. Take the turkey out of the fridge an hour before roasting to allow the meat to relax and come to room temperature, which will make the meat more tender.

Meanwhile, preheat the oven to 230°C/gas mark 8. Remove the giblets from inside the bird's cavity because these can't be cooked with the turkey. Keep them for making turkey stock or gravy. Season the cavity with salt and pepper.

Place all the ingredients for the flavoured butter in a bowl, season with salt and pepper and mix well, using the back of a spoon to blend the ingredients together. Using clean hands, smear the butter mixture all over the turkey as well as underneath the skin.

Add the stuffing to the cavity of the turkey, ensuring that it is only half-filled to allow hot air to circulate and the turkey to cook more evenly.

Line the roasting tray first with the shallots, carrots, garlic, thyme, sage and clementines, then place the stuffed turkey on top. This will flavour the turkey even more during the roasting process.

Roast the turkey for 45 minutes. Then reduce the oven temperature to 180°C/gas mark 4, remove the turkey from the oven and baste the bird with the juices from the pan. Cover the turkey loosely with foil, return to the oven and roast for 3½ hours, continuing to baste the turkey every 45 minutes.

Check to see if the turkey is cooked by inserting a skewer into the thickest part of the thigh – the juices should run clear. Once you have removed the turkey from the oven, leave it to rest for 30 minutes, covered with a loose tent of foil to keep it warm, before carving and serving. This will allow the juices to redistribute themselves, resulting in tastier meat.

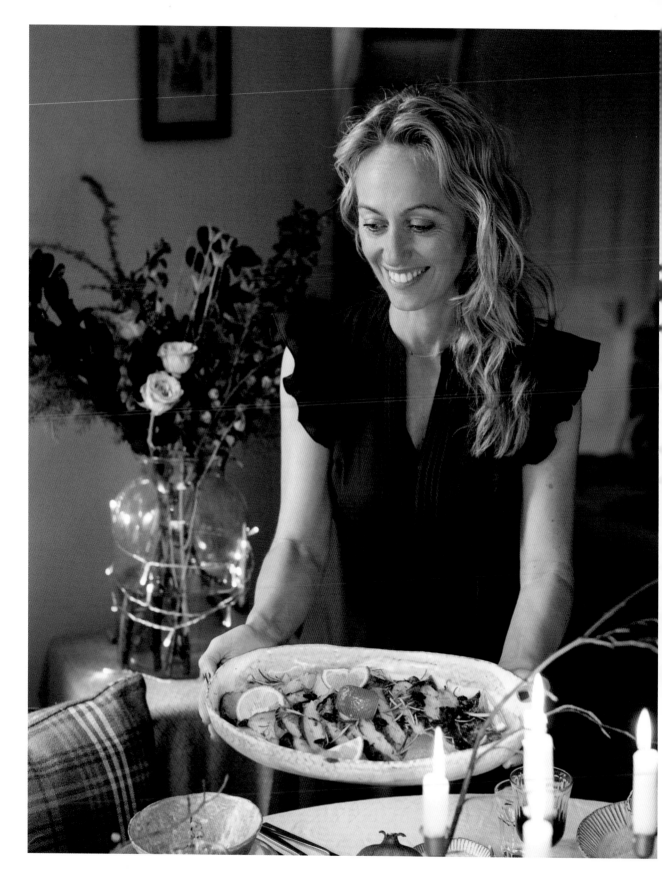

Sweet Potato, Bacon & Pecan Stuffing

SERVES 8

50g salted butter

60g rindless smoked bacon rashers, chopped

1 small onion, finely diced

2 celery sticks, finely diced

2 garlic cloves, crushed

800g sweet potatoes, diced

2 tablespoons maple syrup

300g fresh white breadcrumbs

60g pecan nuts, chopped

50g dried cranberries

100ml hot chicken or turkey stock

2 teaspoons finely chopped thyme leaves

sea salt and freshly ground black pepper

If you want to cook the stuffing separately from the turkey, preheat the oven to 180°C/gas mark 4.

Place a saucepan over a medium heat and add the butter. Once the butter has melted, stir in the bacon and cook for 2 minutes, then add the onion, celery and garlic and cook for a further 3 minutes. Stir in the sweet potatoes and maple syrup and cook for a further 2–3 minutes.

Place the breadcrumbs in a baking dish, followed by the pecans, dried cranberries, stock and thyme, and season with salt and pepper. Add the sweet potato mixture and mix all the ingredients until well combined.

Bake the stuffing for 30 minutes until well browned on top.

Pork Tenderloin Filled with Butternut Squash & Hazelnuts served with Mashed Celeriac

SERVES 4

I love pork loins as they are so easy to cook and work with. In the autumn, I also use blackberries, and apples instead of the butternut squash. You can use this filling for a bigger piece of pork – just double up the recipe. And you can get this all prepared a day ahead so it's a really great stress-free main course.

400g pork tenderloin (fillet)

8 pancetta slices or rindless streaky bacon rashers

butter, for greasing

sea salt and freshly ground black pepper

FOR THE STUFFING

400g butternut squash, peeled, deseeded and diced

50g blanched hazelnuts, finely chopped

1 red onion, finely diced

6 sage leaves, finely chopped

25g fresh white breadcrumbs

50g butter, melted

2 garlic cloves, crushed

FOR THE MASHED CELERIAC

700g celeriac, peeled and cut into chunks

100ml single cream

50g butter

½ teaspoon freshly grated nutmeg

Preheat the oven to 200°C/gas mark 6.

Start by making the stuffing. Place all the ingredients in a large bowl, season with salt and pepper and mix together well.

Butterfly the pork tenderloin by making a slit down its length, cutting just deep enough so that you can open the loin up to lie flat like a book; don't cut all the way through.

Arrange the pancetta or bacon side by side on a lightly greased, large baking tray, then place the pork on top. Spoon the stuffing mixture onto the meat and spread evenly. Close up the tenderloin bit by bit by stretching the pancetta or bacon and using it to wrap around and seal the pork, working all the way along its length so that you end up with a big parcel.

Roast the pork for 25 minutes.

While the pork finishes roasting, make the mashed celeriac. Place the celeriac in a saucepan and cover with cold water. Bring to the boil over a high heat, then reduce to a simmer and cook for 15 minutes or until the celeriac is tender.

Add the cream, butter and nutmeg to a saucepan and warm together over a low heat. Pour the cream mixture over the cooked celeriac, season with salt and pepper and mash together.

Once the pork is cooked, remove from the oven and leave to rest for 15 minutes, tented with foil to keep it warm. Slice the pork and place on a warmed platter, then spoon the mashed celeriac around the pork.

Weekend Fondue with Bread & Pickles

SERVES 4

Cheese fondue is such a fun dish to share with friends and family, especially during the winter months as it is so warming. I love to serve this in the middle of the table in my big Le Creuset casserole dish that I have had for years but if you have a proper fondue set all the better. Dipping in pickles and chunks of bread to scoop up the melting silky cheese is utter winter heaven!

300ml dry white wine

2 garlic cloves, finely chopped

320g Emmental cheese, grated

480g good-quality Gruyère cheese, grated

150g Reblochon cheese

2 teaspoons kirsch (optional)

whole nutmeg, for grating

TO SERVE

sourdough bread, cubed

pickles, such as pickled gherkins, onions and cucumbers

Heat the wine with the garlic in a deep, heavy-based saucepan over a low heat until it begins to simmer.

Add the Emmental, a little at a time, whisking or stirring vigorously and leaving it to melt after each addition before adding more. Repeat the process with the Gruyère, followed by the Reblochon, continuing to stir until smooth.

Stir in the kirsch, if using, followed by a good grating of nutmeg.

Transfer the fondue mixture to a fondue set or heatproof pan set over a tea light and serve with sourdough bread cubes and pickles.

Fish Pie with Dubliner Cheese Rösti Topping

SERVES 2

This is the ultimate fish pie – I promise you! I cook regularly on *Sunday Brunch* and last winter I cooked this dish. I was inundated with viewers sending me their pictures of this fish pie from their kitchens at home, so this is definitely my most celebrated TV recipe to date! The smoky, creamy base of the pie topped with the crispy potato and cheese rösti on top is the perfect texture combination. You can get the base made a day ahead, and then prepare the rösti on the day. Also feel free to swap out the fish for any meaty fish that you like and leave out the cheese in the potato rösti if you prefer.

450g floury potatoes, such as Maris Piper

50g aged Dubliner cheese

250g skinless smoked haddock fillet

250g skinless salmon fillet

100g raw peeled prawns

400ml full-fat milk

1 shallot, peeled and halved

1 bay leaf

1 teaspoon black peppercorns

75g butter, softened

50g plain flour

2 teaspoons Dijon mustard

2 tablespoons chopped dill

sea salt and freshly ground black pepper

Preheat the oven to 200°C/gas mark 6.

Peel the potatoes, then grate using the large holes on a box grater. Place the grated potatoes in a bowl of cold water to stop them from turning brown.

Grate the cheese using the same side of the grater and set aside separately.

Place the smoked haddock, salmon and prawns in a saucepan, pour over the milk and drop in the shallot, bay leaf and peppercorns. Cook over a low heat for 5 minutes, then drain, reserving the poaching milk but discarding the onion, bay leaf and peppercorns. Transfer the fish to a baking dish.

Melt 50g of the butter in a saucepan over a medium heat. Stir in the flour and cook, continuing to stir, until a paste (roux) forms. Then gradually add the reserved fish poaching milk as well as the mustard, whisking constantly, and cook until you have a smooth, thickened sauce. Season with salt and pepper and stir in half the dill, then pour the sauce over the fish.

Drain the grated potatoes and pat with a clean tea-towel until they are completely dry. Mix the grated potatoes and the remaining dill into the grated cheese and season with salt, then scatter over the fish and the sauce.

Melt the remaining butter in a saucepan and brush over the top of the pie to ensure that the top gets really crispy. Bake for 20 minutes or until golden brown.

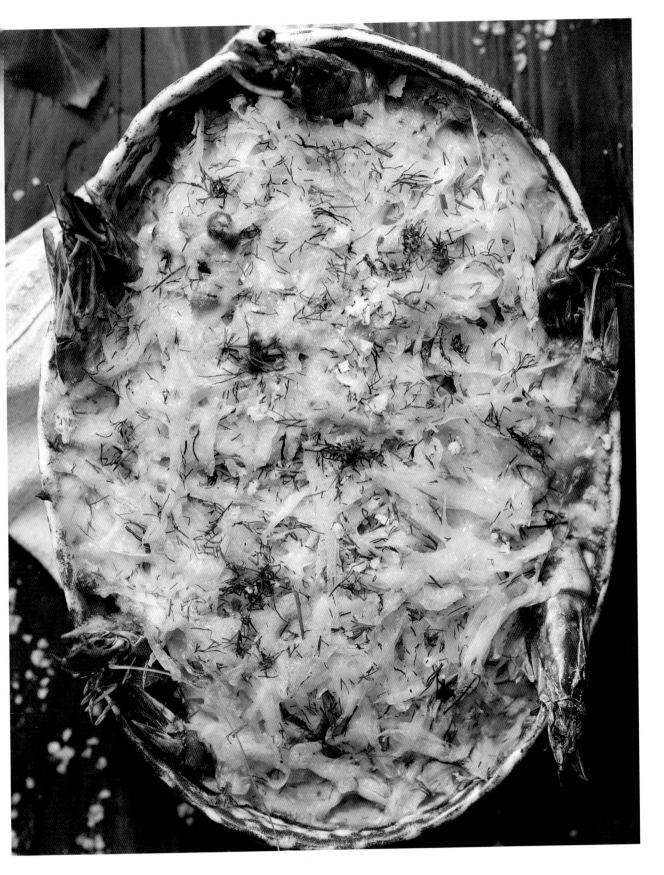

Plum Pudding Ice Cream

SERVES 6

Making your own ice cream is so simple – it really is just a case of placing all the ingredients in a pot over a low heat, stirring, freezing and whisking every hour or so. You don't need an ice-cream maker. Adding the crumbles of plum pudding gives delicious little surprise bits of juicy fruitiness. It's a light and refreshing dessert to serve during the Christmas period and also a great way to use up any leftover pudding from the holidays. The grated zest of an orange would also be a lovely addition.

250ml double cream

250ml full-fat milk

150g caster sugar

1 vanilla pod

5 egg yolks

150g plum pudding, crumbled

Pour the cream and milk into a saucepan, place over a medium heat and stir in the sugar. Slit the vanilla pod down its length with a small sharp knife, scoop out the tiny black seeds and stir into the saucepan. Reduce the heat and stir until all the sugar has dissolved, then remove the pan from the heat.

Place the eggs yolks in a large bowl and beat to combine, then slowly whisk in the warmed cream and milk mixture. Return the mixture to the saucepan, place over a low heat and stir until it thickens to a custard consistency.

Remove the pan from the heat, pour the ice cream mixture into a freezerproof container and leave to cool completely.

Freeze the ice cream mixture for 2 hours, then remove from the freezer and stir well with a fork until you have a smooth consistency (this will prevent any ice crystals forming). Return to the freezer for 30 minutes and then repeat the stirring process. Freeze for a further 30 minutes, then fold in 100g of the crumbled plum pudding (reserve the remainder for serving) and return to the freezer for a final 2 hours of freezing.

Serve the ice cream with the remaining crumble of plum pudding on top.

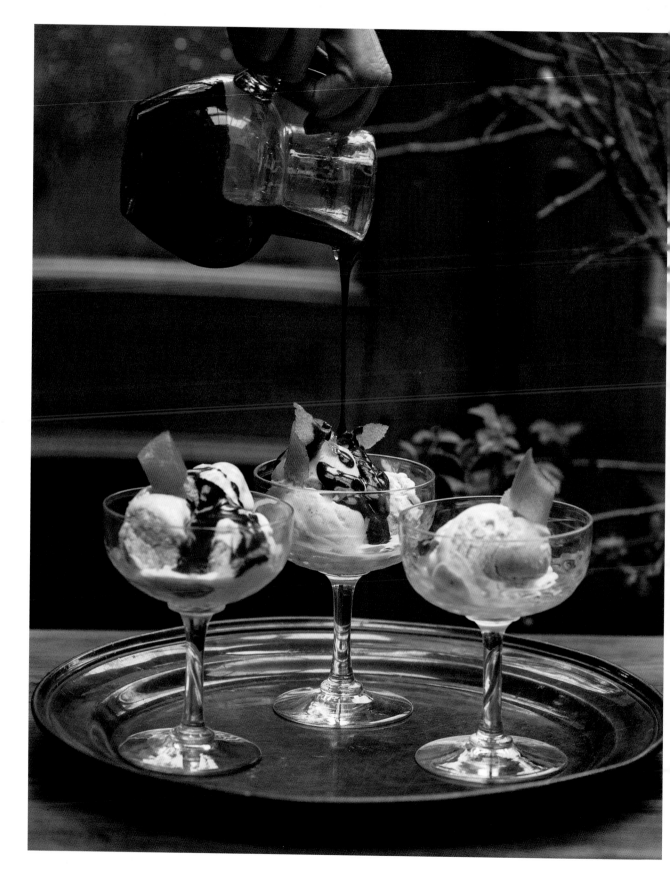

Hot Chocolate Affogato with Candied Orange Peel

SERVES 4

When I lived in Italy, affogato was something I served for dessert all the time. It's everything you want in a dessert – refreshing chilled ice cream warmed with hot espresso coffee. This version is a bit more special with the rich, silky melted dark chocolate and the festive fresh flavour of orange. It's one of the easiest desserts to make and it looks and tastes fantastic!

200ml double cream

200g dark chocolate (70% cocoa solids), chopped (or use nibs)

100ml strong espresso coffee

grated zest of 1 orange

8 scoops of good-quality vanilla ice cream

8 strips of candied orange peel

Place the cream, dark chocolate, espresso and orange zest in a saucepan over a low heat. Heat, stirring, until the chocolate has melted into the cream.

Add two scoops of vanilla ice cream to four chilled glasses and place each on a saucer along with a spoon and two strips of candied orange peel. Pour the chocolate and espresso sauce into a warmed jug.

Bring everything to the table and assemble the affogato in front of everyone, as the ice cream will melt once you pour over the sauce and it looks great too! Arrange two strips of candied orange peel on top of each serving and pour the hot chocolate and espresso sauce over the ice cream.

Cashel Blue Oat Cheesecake with Irish Honey

MAKES 1 CHEESECAKE

Blue cheese is at its best during the winter months and I think we all love smoky creamy cheese around this time of the year. If you're not a fan of blue cheese, you can make this dish with cream cheese, but if you are doing so then I would leave out the thyme. The blue cheese together with the earthy flavour of the fresh thyme, sweetened by the honey and a base of crunchy oatcakes is absolutely delicious! It's halfway between savoury and sweet, so there's no need to serve a cheeseboard afterwards. You can make this a few days ahead and it will last about a week in the fridge. But take it out of the fridge at least an hour before serving so it comes to room temperature.

200g oatcakes

50g walnuts, toasted

100g butter, melted, plus extra for greasing

500g cream cheese

100ml soured cream

3 eggs, lightly beaten

50g plain flour, seasoned

250g Cashel Blue cheese, crumbled

1 tablespoon chopped thyme leaves

2 teaspoons clear Irish honey, plus extra to serve

sea salt and freshly ground black pepper

Preheat the oven to 140°C/gas mark 1. Grease and line the base and sides of a 20cm springform cake tin with baking paper.

Add the oatcakes and toasted walnuts to a food-processor and process to crumbs. Tip into a bowl, add the melted butter with a pinch of salt and a grinding of pepper and mix together well. Transfer the buttery crumbs to the prepared tin, using the back of a spoon to spread and press them into an even, well-compacted layer over the base and sides. Chill in the fridge for at least 30 minutes until firm and cold.

To make the filling, beat the cream cheese in a bowl with a wooden spoon until smooth. Add the soured cream and beat again. Gradually pour in the beaten eggs, beating after each addition, until fully combined.

Sift the seasoned flour over the cream cheese mixture and gently fold it in, then fold in the blue cheese, thyme and honey until well combined.

Scrape the mixture into the chilled oatcake case and smooth the top. Bake for 1 hour or until just set with the tiniest wobble in the centre. Turn off the heat and leave the cheesecake to cool completely in the oven. Serve with a drizzle of extra honey.

Chocolate Pecan Brownie Trifle with Orange Blossom Cream

MAKES 1 TRIFLE

FOR THE CHOCOLATE BROWNIE

300g good-quality dark chocolate (70% cocoa solids), broken into chunks

100g butter, chopped, plus extra for greasing

4 eggs

200g light muscovado sugar

200g plain flour

100g pecan nuts, roughly chopped

FOR THE CHOCOLATE MOUSSE

250g good-quality dark chocolate (70% cocoa solids), broken into chunks

2 tablespoons cocoa powder

100ml single cream

2 tablespoons orange blossom water

6 egg whites

120g caster sugar

TO FINISH THE TRIFLE

500ml whipping cream

1 tablespoon orange blossom water

50g pecan nuts, chopped

50g dark chocolate curls or flakes

This is a showstopping dessert to serve at Christmas or on special occasions. I always slightly under-bake the brownie as it can become dry so fast – you can also swap out the pecans for hazelnuts or almonds if you wish. If you haven't ever used orange blossom water before, please go and buy a bottle – it adds such a magical, delicate floral flavour to any cream. You can serve this in individual glasses or in a large glass trifle bowl. Add soft berries to the top if you wish.

Start by making the brownie. Preheat the oven to 180°C/gas mark 4. Grease a 30 x 20cm baking tin.

Melt the chocolate and butter in a heatproof bowl set over a saucepan of simmering water, stirring gently until smooth and combined (don't let the base of the bowl touch the water). Set aside to cool slightly.

Place the eggs and sugar in a large bowl or the bowl of a stand mixer and whisk together until pale and fluffy. Whisk the chocolate and butter mixture into the egg mixture, then gently fold in the flour and chopped pecans.

Pour the mixture into the tin, smooth the surface, then bake for 25 minutes or until firm around the edges but slightly soft in the middle. Leave to cool in the tin for 10 minutes, then turn out onto a wire rack to cool completely.

While the brownie is cooling, make the chocolate mousse. Melt the chocolate in a heatproof bowl set over a pan of simmering water (don't let the base of the bowl touch the water). Once melted, stir in the cocoa, then remove from the heat and stir in the single cream and orange blossom water.

Place the egg whites in a very clean and dry large bowl or the bowl of the stand mixer and use an electric hand whisk or the whisk attachment on the stand mixer to whisk until firm peaks form. Gradually add the sugar, a tablespoon at a time, whisking constantly until the mixture is stiff. Gently fold it into the cooled chocolate mixture.

To finish the trifle, pour the whipping cream into a bowl, add the orange blossom water and whisk together until softly whipped.

To assemble the trifle, break the brownie into pieces and add half to your trifle bowl. Then spoon half the chocolate mousse on top, followed by half the orange blossom cream. Repeat with the remaining brownie, mousse and cream, then sprinkle the chopped pecans and chocolate curls or flakes on top.

Tarte Tatin with Thyme

SERVES 6

I experimented with this recipe so many times in my little kitchen in London to get the perfect result. It's such an easy recipe to make, but you need to follow the steps to make it perfectly. Cook the caramel until it is light golden and then immediately place the apples on top followed by the puff pastry, and then put it straight into the oven. You can make it a few hours ahead and just let it sit on the side, then reheat it in a low oven. I love to serve mine with a dollop of crème fraîche. Try swapping out the apples for plums, pears or peaches at other times of the year.

165g caster sugar

100ml water

65g unsalted butter

2 teaspoons chopped thyme leaves, plus 6 sprigs, to decorate

4 dessert apples, peeled, cored and quartered

3 sheets of ready-rolled puff pastry, defrosted if frozen

crème fraîche, to serve

Preheat the oven to 180°C/gas mark 4.

Place a cast-iron or ovenproof frying pan over a low heat, add the sugar and water and heat, stirring, until the sugar has dissolved.

Increase the heat to high and simmer for 12–14 minutes or until the syrup is a light golden brown colour. Then stir in the butter and chopped thyme and cook for a further 2–3 minutes or until you have a caramel consistency.

Arrange the apples cut-side up in the pan and slightly overlapping to ensure that the caramel is completely covered with the apples.

Place the puff pastry sheets on top of each other and roll out so that they combine and are large enough to cover the apples in the pan, with enough excess to tuck in around the sides of the pan.

Place the pastry on top of the apples and fold the edges downwards to tuck in the apples, then use a sharp knife to make three small slits in the centre of the pastry top.

Transfer the pan to the oven and bake for 45 minutes until the pastry is golden brown.

Remove the pan from the oven. Wearing oven gloves, carefully invert the tart onto your serving dish. Cut into wedges, decorate each serving with a thyme sprig and serve with a dollop of crème fraîche.

Star Anise & Orange Rice Pudding

SERVES 6

Creamy rice pudding infused with the aniseed flavour of star anise and given sweetness and zestiness by the orange is a delicious spoonful of flavour and texture. There are so many variations that I make to this recipe – you can add dried fruit, such as raisins, sultanas, dates, apricots or cranberries with a sprinkle of ground cinnamon for a very festive dessert. You can serve it warm, at room temperature or chilled – all are equally good. If you make it a day ahead, then loosen it up before serving in a saucepan with some warmed milk and stir until the consistency is smooth again.

10g butter

80g pudding (short-grain) rice

55g caster sugar

100g sultanas

3 star anise

1 teaspoon freshly grated nutmeg

800ml milk

grated zest and juice of 1 orange

3 satsumas, peeled and segmented

Preheat the oven to 160°C/gas mark 3. Grease a 1.2-litre baking dish with the butter.

Place the rice, sugar, sultanas, star anise and nutmeg in the greased baking dish and mix together well. Then add the milk and orange zest and juice and stir to mix.

Bake the rice pudding for 1½ hours, stirring a couple of times during the cooking time – a skin will form on the top of the pudding while baking.

Remove the rice pudding from the oven. Scrape back the skin and remove the star anise, then rinse and dry them, cut in half and use for decorating your puddings.

Fill six glasses one-third of the way with the rice pudding and top with satsuma segments, then repeat the layers until you have filled each glass. Alternatively, you can layer the rice pudding and satsumas in the same way in a large dessert bowl. Decorate with the star anise and serve at room temperature.

Date & Almond Bread & Butter Pudding

SERVES 6

Bread and butter pudding is a childhood favourite, my mum would make it using up all the leftover bread. Now I keep bread back to use for the pudding! You can make this with brioche too, which is a much richer result. The dates and almonds get blended together to make a natural nutty caramel paste that gets whipped into the eggy milk mixture. In the oven it becomes soufflé-like because of the eggs and milk – so it's fluffy and delicious. Serve with a dollop of softly whipped cream and a dusting of ground cinnamon if you like.

250ml milk

250ml single cream

100g caster sugar

4 eggs

1 teaspoon vanilla extract

1 tablespoon ground cinnamon

400g dried pitted dates

100ml water

12 slices of white bread, cut into triangles

100g butter, softened

60g blanched almonds, finely chopped

softly whipped cream or ice cream, to serve

Preheat the oven to 160°C/gas mark 3.

Place a saucepan over a medium heat, add the milk, cream and sugar and mix together. Heat, stirring, until the sugar has dissolved, then set aside to cool.

Whisk the eggs in a large bowl, then stir in the vanilla extract and cinnamon. Whisk into the cooled milk mixture.

Place the dates in a blender or food-processer with the water and blend to a purée. Then add the date mixture to the custard mixture and mix together.

Spread the triangles of bread with the butter. Arrange them, overlapping, in a baking dish, then pour over the date and custard mixture. Use your hands to push the bread gently into the custard mixture so that it is completely immersed.

Scatter the chopped almonds over the top of the pudding, then bake for 45 minutes. Serve with softly whipped cream or ice cream.

Sparkling Rhubarb Cocktail

This is such a pretty-looking cocktail and one I love to serve before suppers or at a party when the first of the rhubarb comes into season. Make the rhubarb syrup the day before and decant into a pretty glass jug, alongside a bottle of chilled sparkling wine on a tray with glasses. I like to set this up in the garden, on a table with flowers alongside one of my nibbles to create a lovely occasion.

SERVES 8

750g rhubarb, trimmed and chopped

150g caster sugar

grated zest and juice of 1 orange

chilled sparkling wine, to top up

To make the rhubarb syrup, place the rhubarb, sugar and orange zest and juice in a saucepan and add a splash of water. Bring to the boil, then reduce the heat to low and simmer gently, uncovered, for 10–15 minutes until the rhubarb is very soft.

Strain the syrup through a fine sieve into a jug, pressing the rhubarb to extract all the juice, then leave to cool.

Pour a little of the rhubarb syrup into each glass and top up with chilled sparkling wine.

Fig Leaf & Thyme Cocktail

SERVES 12

FOR THE FIG LEAF & THYME SYRUP

350g caster sugar

500ml water

8 fresh fig leaves, thoroughly washed

8 thyme sprigs

FOR THE COCKTAIL

6 lemons, halved, for squeezing

600ml gin

1.2 litres soda water

ice cubes, to serve

The leaves from the fig tree that I have in my garden flop over the entrance to the house, so I am welcomed by them every day in the summer and autumn. There is a lovely soft figgy smell to them, so one day I decided to clip them and make a syrup from them with a little thyme, also from my garden. The result was this wonderful figgy aromatic syrup that is so delicious in this cocktail.

To make the fig leaf and thyme syrup, place the sugar and measured water in a saucepan over a high heat and stir until the sugar has dissolved. Stir in the fig leaves and thyme sprigs, reduce the heat and simmer, uncovered, for 1 hour.

Strain the syrup through a sieve into a jug, discard the fig leaves and thyme and leave to cool.

For the cocktail, place a couple of ice cubes in each glass, followed by the juice of $\frac{1}{2}$ lemon. Then pour in a double measure (50ml) of gin, 3 tablespoons of the fig leaf and thyme syrup and 100ml soda water. Stir and serve.

The Smoky

SERVES 2 (WITH A TOP-UP FOR BOTH!)

125ml Irish whiskey

4 dashes of Angostura bitters

juice of 1 lemon

juice of ½ orange

5 tablespoons sugar syrup

2 organic or free-range egg whites

ice cubes

2 orange slices, to garnish (optional)

My boyfriend and I decided we wanted to create a house cocktail – one that we would go back to in-between seasons and that our friends could look forward to having when they came for supper. It was a fun weekend experimenting with this cocktail, full of lots of testing and laughing... We often just make it for ourselves on a Friday night after a long work week, followed by a little dance! It's similar to an Old Fashioned – I love the egg white in it as it lightens it all up and gives a delicious creamy texture. It is my all-time favourite cocktail and has become a signature drink at all my suppers at home.

Place the whiskey, Angostura bitters, lemon and orange juices, sugar syrup and egg whites in a cocktail shaker with some ice cubes. Shake for 1 minute.

Pour into two chilled coupe glasses, then garnish each with an orange slice.

Lime, Mint & Sea Salt Cocktail

SERVES 6

FOR THE LIME & MINT SYRUP

300g caster sugar

700ml water

6 mint sprigs, plus 6 half sprigs to serve

grated zest of 4 limes

FOR THE SODA

juice of 4 limes, plus 2 wedges and 6 slices to serve

gin

soda water

sea salt and ice, to serve

This is my version of a mojito – salty, sweet, refreshingly cooling with mint, and zesty from the fresh limes. The syrup is so simple to make, and will last in an airtight container for up to two weeks, so you can make it well ahead.

To make the lime and mint syrup, place all the ingredients in a saucepan over a medium heat and gently bring to the boil, stirring until the sugar has dissolved.

Remove the pan from the heat and leave the syrup to infuse for 1 hour.

For the soda, strain the syrup through a sieve into a jug, discard the mint and stir in the lime juice.

When you are ready to serve, spread a layer of sea salt on a saucer. Run a lime wedge around the outside of the rim of each glass and then roll the rim in the sea salt so that it is completely covered. First fill each glass halfway with ice and add a lime slice and half a mint sprig. Then fill the glasses one-quarter of the way with the lime and mint mixture, one-quarter with gin, and the remaining half with soda water. Stir and serve.

Rosemary & Lemon Gin Soda

FOR THE ROSEMARY & LEMON
SYRUP

250g caster sugar

300ml water

3 rosemary sprigs, plus 6,
to serve

FOR THE SODA

juice of 6 lemons

gin

soda water

ice cubes and 6 lemon slices,
to serve

This cocktail is best served in small tumbler glasses with a thin slice of lemon and a sprig of fresh rosemary, which can also be used as a stirrer. You can serve a non-alchocolic option by just leaving out the gin and adding extra soda water. It's also great with vodka.

To make the rosemary and lemon syrup, place the syrup ingredients in a saucepan over a medium heat and gently bring to the boil, stirring until the sugar has dissolved.

Remove the pan from the heat and leave the syrup to infuse for 2 hours.

For the soda, strain the syrup through a sieve into a jug, discard the rosemary and stir in the lemon juice.

When you are ready to serve, fill each glass halfway with ice cubes and add a lemon slice and a rosemary sprig. Fill the glasses one-quarter of the way with the rosemary and lemon mixture, one-quarter with gin, and the remaining half with soda water. Stir and serve.

Blackberry & Rosemary Cocktail

SERVES 8

FOR THE BLACKBERRY SYRUP

200g caster sugar

480ml water

450g fresh blackberries,
plus 8, to serve

FOR THE COCKTAIL

120ml fresh lemon juice

gin

soda water

ice and 8 rosemary sprigs, to serve

When blackberries are in season, there is nothing more special than spending the weekend picking the berries from the hedgerows. There are so many fun things to make from them – this cocktail being one. The blackberry syrup is delicious with fresh rosemary, but you could also use fresh mint. Vodka works well too, and it's also a great non-alcoholic cocktail – just add more soda and leave out the alcohol.

To make the blackberry syrup, place the syrup ingredients in a saucepan over a medium heat and gently bring to the boil, stirring until the sugar has dissolved. Remove the pan from the heat and leave the syrup to cool.

Stir the lemon juice into the cooled blackberry syrup.

When you are ready to serve, fill each glass halfway with ice and add a rosemary sprig and a blackberry. Fill the glasses one-quarter of the way with the blackberry and lemon juice mixture, one-quarter with gin, and the remaining half with soda water. Stir and serve.

Butternut Squash & Harissa Hummus

SERVES 6

400g butternut squash, peeled, deseeded and cut into chunks

3 garlic cloves, unpeeled

100ml water

3 tablespoons tahini paste

2 tablespoons olive oil, plus extra for drizzling

1 tablespoon harissa, plus extra for drizzling

400g can chickpeas, rinsed and drained

sea salt and freshly ground black pepper

TO SERVE

2 wedges of lemon

1 teaspoon pumpkin seeds

I came up with this recipe for a Thanksgiving special on *The Marilyn Denis Show*. You can serve this with toasted sourdough, crispbreads, vegetable crudités or spiced pittas. To make the spiced pittas, whisk together 2 teaspoons of smoked paprika with the juice of ½ lemon, 50ml olive oil and a sprinkle of sea salt. Cut the pittas into small triangles and brush them with the paprika oil, then transfer onto a baking sheet and into a hot oven for 6–7 minutes until they are toasted.

Preheat the oven to 180°C/gas mark 4.

Place the butternut squash chunks and whole garlic cloves in a roasting tray, season well with salt and pepper and add the water. Cover the tray with foil and bake for about 45 minutes until the squash is tender. Remove from the oven and leave to cool.

Squeeze the roasted garlic from their skins into a blender or food-processor along with the squash and any juices from the roasting tray. Add all the remaining ingredients, season with salt and blend to a paste.

Scrape the hummus into a bowl. Drizzle with extra harissa, olive oil and pumpkin seeds. Serve with a couple of lemon wedges on the side.

Tuscan White Bean & Rosemary Dip

SERVES 4

400g can cannellini beans, rinsed and drained

5 tablespoons extra virgin olive oil

1 teaspoon finely chopped rosemary leaves

1 garlic clove, crushed

juice of 1 lemon

1 teaspoon cayenne pepper

sea salt and freshly ground black pepper

vegetable crudités or breadsticks, to serve

A great handy dip recipe to have up your sleeve as it uses mainly store cupboard ingredients and takes less than 5 minutes to make! When I am serving it, I like to add a sprinkle of chopped toasted almonds on top, a good drizzle of extra virgin olive oil and some finely chopped fresh rosemary – it adds great texture and it looks so beautiful. You can make this up a day ahead and keep it in the fridge.

Place all the ingredients in a blender or food-processor, season with salt and pepper and blend until smooth.

Serve the dip with vegetable crudités or breadsticks.

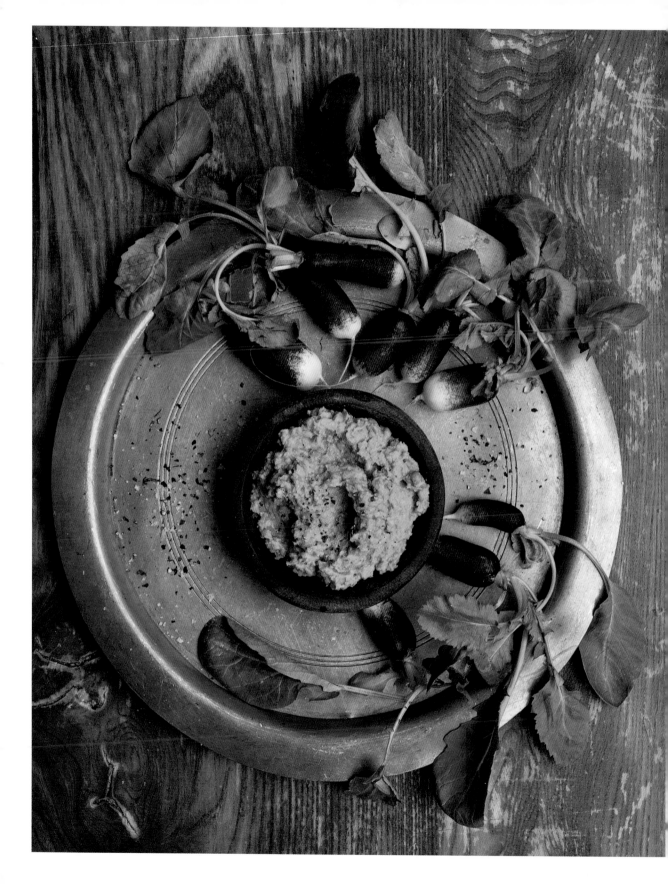

Spring Pea Guacamole with Radishes

SERVES 4

1 ripe avocado

200g peas, podded fresh weight or frozen, defrosted if frozen

2 tablespoons chopped mint

½ teaspoon dried chilli flakes

1 tablespoon crème fraîche

grated zest and juice of 1 lime

sea salt and freshly ground black pepper

12 whole radishes, with leaves on, to serve

The colours and taste of this dish are deliciously fresh and are the very essence of spring. The peas bring a lovely sweetness to the avocado and it's all lightly heated with the chilli. The fresh crunch of the radishes with this pea guacamole is so good and they look so beautiful. You could use other vegetables, like baby carrots, celery, spring onions, sugar snaps or chicory leaves. This is best made on the day as the peas can slightly lose their colour in the fridge overnight – but it only takes a few minutes to make, so it's very stress free!

Cut the avocado in half lengthways and remove the stone, then peel the avocado halves and add to a blender or food-processor.

Add all the remaining ingredients except the radishes to the blender or food-processor, season with salt and pepper and blend for about 1 minute until smooth.

Scoop the guacamole into a serving bowl and serve with the radishes.

Spiced Candied Pecans

SERVES 4

2 teaspoons sea salt

½ teaspoon dried thyme

½ teaspoon granulated sugar

¼ teaspoon freshly ground black pepper

¼ teaspoon cayenne pepper

50g butter, melted

200g raw pecan nuts

These are gorgeous to serve with cocktails. Sweet, salty and spicy flavours all coating the pecans; you could use almonds or cashew nuts too. I also love making these in big batches to give as gifts – they look so lovely in small Kilner jars with a handwritten label. They will last for a couple of weeks in an airtight container.

Preheat the oven to 180°C/gas mark 4, and position a shelf in the middle of the oven. Line a baking sheet with baking paper and set aside.

Place all the ingredients except the butter and pecans in a large bowl and stir to combine. Pour in the melted butter and stir until incorporated, then add the nuts and stir until evenly coated.

Spread the nuts out in a single layer on the lined baking sheet and roast for 15 minutes, stirring once, until golden brown.

Remove from the oven and leave to cool on the baking sheet, then transfer to a dish and serve.

Smoked Salmon Pâté

SERVES 4

250g smoked salmon, roughly chopped

100g cream cheese

50ml crème fraîche

1 teaspoon capers

1 teaspoon finely chopped dill

juice of 1 lemon

sea salt and freshly ground black pepper

very thin slices of bread, toasted, or crackers, to serve

I have been making this smoked salmon pâté for years and this recipe is a particular favourite of mine. I love serving it simply on very thinly sliced sourdough toast or some nice crispy thin crackers. It also works perfectly as a starter. If you like smoked mackerel, then you can use this exact recipe and just swap out the smoked salmon. I sometimes fold thinly sliced gherkins into the pâté for added flavour and texture. It's so incredibly simple to make, just pop all the ingredients in a food-processor and blend!

Place all the ingredients (except the bread) in a blender or food-processor, season with salt and pepper and blend until you have a smooth consistency.

Serve the pâté with very thin toast or crackers.

Smoked Paprika Aioli

MAKES 250ML

2 egg yolks

1 tablespoon white wine vinegar

1 teaspoon Dijon mustard

120ml extra virgin olive oil

120ml vegetable oil

juice of ½ lemon

½ garlic clove, crushed

1 teaspoon smoked paprika

sea salt and freshly ground black pepper

Put the egg yolks into a bowl, add the vinegar and mustard and lightly whisk them all together.

Whisk the extra virgin olive and vegetable oils together, then slowly add to the egg yolk mixture, whisking constantly, beginning with a few drops at a time and then in a thin, steady stream when the mixture begins to get thick and creamy.

When all the oil is incorporated, stir in the lemon juice, garlic and smoked paprika, and season with salt and pepper.

Aged Dubliner Cheese Oat Croquettes with Smoked Paprika Aioli

MAKES 10 CROQUETTES

Cheesy, fluffy croquettes rolled in crunchy oats and then dipped in a lightly spiced aioli is such a delicious nibble to serve before a supper party or as a canapé during a party. You can swap out the Dubliner cheese for one of your favourite Cheddars or any good cheese that melts well. I use oats in the crust, but you could use just breadcrumbs if you wish and add in some finely ground nuts, like almonds. These can be prepared a day ahead and chilled then cooked off on the day that you are serving. The croquettes freeze very well too.

3 potatoes, steamed, peeled and mashed (see page 45)

100g aged Dubliner cheese, grated

2 teaspoons Dijon mustard

2 teaspoons finely chopped flat-leaf parsley

50g fine fresh breadcrumbs

50g porridge oats

1 egg, beaten

vegetable oil, for frying

sea salt and freshly ground black pepper

Smoked Paprika Aioli, to serve (see opposite)

Place the mashed potatoes, cheese, mustard and parsley in a large bowl. Season with salt and pepper and mix together well.

Use a dessertspoon to scoop small amounts of the potato mixture, form into balls the size of a table tennis ball and place on a tray.

Mix the breadcrumbs and porridge oats together in a bowl, then spread out on a large plate.

Using a pastry brush, paint the croquettes all over with the beaten egg. Then one by one, gently roll the croquettes in the crumb mixture to coat.

Pour a shallow depth of vegetable oil into a large frying pan and place over a medium-high heat.

Once the oil is hot, add the croquettes and fry for a few minutes, turning once, until golden. Alternatively, bake them on a baking sheet in an oven preheated to 200°C/gas mark 6 for 15 minutes.

Serve the croquettes hot with the smoked paprika aioli.

Pistachio & Rosewater Florentines

These are a staple after-supper treat at most of my suppers. They are without any doubt the most delicious chocolate recipe that I have made and they are so simple to make! It's literally a case of melting, stirring, spooning, sprinkling and chilling. They take about 15 minutes to make. I sometimes serve them placed on top of a scoop of ice cream, like a Philip Treacy hat! There are lots of variations (but this rosewater and pistachio is the best) – orange blossom water with almonds, espresso coffee with hazelnuts or candied orange peel. Make them a day ahead and keep chilled. Try to prepare extra if you have time, as people will gobble them up!

300g dark chocolate (70% cocoa solids), chopped

100g pistachio nuts, finely chopped

1 tablespoon rosewater

10g dried rose petals

Melt the chocolate in a heatproof bowl set over a saucepan of simmering water (don't let the base of the bowl touch the water).

Remove the bowl from the pan and stir half the pistachios and all the rosewater into the melted chocolate.

Place separate dessertspoonfuls of the chocolate mixture onto a sheet of baking paper and form into even-sized rounds.

Sprinkle the remaining pistachios and the dried rose petals on top, then gently press into the melted chocolate. Chill in the fridge for an hour until set.

Chocolate Coconut Truffles

MAKES 40 TRUFFLES

There is nothing quite like a homemade fresh chocolate truffle and they are so simple to make. I roll the truffles in finely chopped coconut flakes; other variations that I roll them in are finely chopped pistachios, hazelnuts or almonds. In the chocolate truffle mixture there are so many delicious flavours I love to add – rosewater, cinnamon, espresso coffee or cream liqueur. I also make them up for gifts during the holiday season. Make this up a day ahead, and remember to take them out of the fridge at least an hour before serving them so that they are at room temperature.

300ml double cream

450g dark chocolate (70% cocoa solids), chopped

60g raw coconut flakes, finely chopped

Pour the cream into a saucepan and bring to a simmer over a medium heat.

Place the chocolate in a heatproof bowl. Pour the hot cream all at once over the chocolate, cover and leave to sit for about 3 minutes. Then gently stir with a spoon until the mixture is smooth and thoroughly blended.

Leave to cool to room temperature, stirring occasionally, then chill in the fridge for 3–4 hours until the ganache is thick and quite stiff.

Line a baking sheet with greaseproof or baking paper, and place the coconut flakes in a bowl. Use a dessertspoon to scoop small amounts of the ganache and then quickly roll between your palms to form into balls.

Dip the chocolate balls into the coconut flakes until each is coated with the coconut.

Place the truffles on the lined baking sheet and chill in the fridge for at least 1 hour. Remove from the fridge an hour before serving.

Mini Rosemary & Sea Salt Butter Cookies

MAKES 24 COOKIES

I developed this recipe for a TV advert campaign in the USA for Kerrygold butter. I had to come up with the perfect buttery cookie and the best flavour combination. After a few days of experimenting with lots of different quantities of butter and various flavours in the end this is what we all agreed on being the perfect buttery cookie. The fresh rosemary adds such a delicious sweet earthy flavour and the sea salt brings that lovely lip-smacking element. I love to make these in little mini versions and serve them with coffee after supper. They are also so cute packaged up as gifts in cellophane bags – tied with a piece of twine and a fresh rosemary sprig.

225g unsalted butter, softened

200g caster sugar

2 teaspoons vanilla extract

1 egg yolk

240g plain flour, plus extra for dusting

2 tablespoons finely chopped rosemary leaves

2 teaspoons sea salt

Place the butter, sugar and vanilla extract in a bowl and beat together until smooth and creamy. Mix in the egg yolk until well incorporated.

Sift in the flour, add the rosemary and sea salt and then mix to combine. Scrape onto a lightly floured work surface and knead just until the dough smooths out.

Transfer the dough to a sheet of clingfilm and roll into a log, then wrap in the clingfilm and chill in the fridge for an hour.

Preheat the oven to 160°C/gas mark 3, and line two large baking sheets with baking paper.

Remove the cookie dough from the fridge, unwrap and cut into slices about 3mm thick. Arrange the slices on the lined baking sheets about 2.5cm apart (they won't be spreading very much, but they need room for air to circulate around them).

Bake for about 12 minutes until only just beginning to turn golden around the edges.

Remove from the oven and leave to cool on the baking sheet, before eating. Store in an airtight container for up to one week.

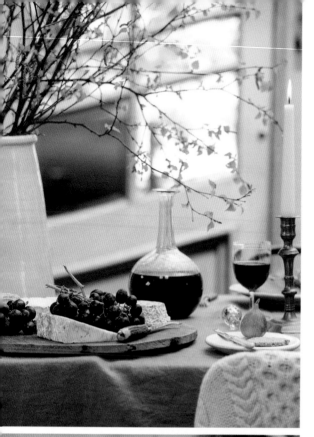

Cheeseboard

HOW TO CREATE A CHEESEBOARD

When I am putting together a large cheeseboard I gather together cheeses that have different textures and flavours. There are five different categories of cheese – soft, fresh, blue, hard and semi-soft, and I usually stick with getting one of each. I like to lay out all my cheeses on a big wooden board before my guests arrive, and place it on a sideboard with a light cotton cloth or tea-towel loosely laid on top – just to protect the cheeses.

I always serve a chutney with my cheeseboard and I have a house Spicy Apple Chutney that I have made for years. I think it's lovely to serve a homemade chutney – have a go at making mine (see opposite). But of course there are lots of interesting chutneys that you can buy, such as onion jam, fig chutney, pear chutney and so on. I also serve slices of dessert apple, as this is a great palate cleanser in-between cheeses, and I also love a big bunch of red grapes as they freshen the palate and their sweetness really complements the cheese. When figs are in season I lay them on my cheeseboard as they go so well with many varieties of cheese.

I serve oatcakes with my cheeses, as they have a wonderful crumbly texture and cereal flavour that is the perfect undertone to all different cheeses. Do try my recipe for Rosemary Oatcakes (see opposite).

When I am having a small supper, I just serve one hero cheese. When it's just one cheese, you can really spend the time selecting something special and finding out about where and how it was made, so that you can share it with your friends over supper.

Remember to you take the cheese out of the fridge at least a couple of hours before serving, to bring the cheese to room temperature, so it will taste its best. And pour a lovely glass of port for all your friends to create the perfect cheese course.

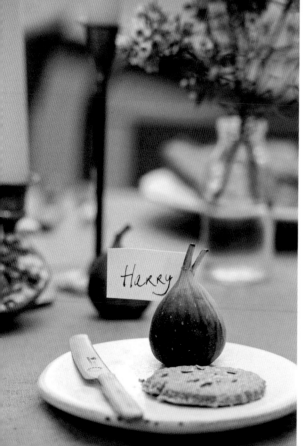

Rosemary Oatcakes

MAKES 20

¼ teaspoon baking powder

180ml warm water

80g butter, melted

250g rolled oats

80g wholemeal flour, plus
extra for dusting

1 tablespoon finely chopped
rosemary

1 teaspoon sea salt

20g caster sugar

Preheat the oven to 180°C/gas mark 4.

Dissolve the baking powder in the warm water and whisk in the melted butter.

Place the oats, flour, rosemary, salt and sugar in a large bowl and mix together.

Pour the liquid into the dry ingredients, stirring as you pour to make a stiff dough.

Lightly dust a clean work surface with a little flour and roll out the dough to about 5mm thick. Cut out 20 x 6cm circles using a pastry cutter.

Arrange on lined baking sheets and bake for 35 minutes until pale golden. Turn the oatcakes over in the oven after 25 minutes. Cool on a wire rack. Store in an airtight container for up to two weeks.

Spicy Apple Chutney

MAKES 12 X 250ML JARS

3kg cooking apples, peeled,
quartered and cored

3 onions

80g butter

600g dark soft brown sugar

20 cloves

2 tablespoons chilli powder

2 tablespoons ground turmeric

12.5cm piece of fresh ginger,
peeled and grated

600ml cider vinegar

sea salt and freshly ground
black pepper

I first started making this chutney to sell at the farmers' markets in Ireland over 16 years ago. It is the best chutney I have ever made and there is always a pot in my kitchen! The perfect time to make it is when apples are in season, so that is when I make big batches – usually about 30 or 40 jars. It lasts for about six months stored in a cool, dark place, so you can enjoy it throughout the whole year. The flavours are sweet and spicy – so work perfectly with cheeses, pâtés and cold meats.

Chop the apples into small chunks and dice the onions.

Place a large saucepan over a low heat and melt the butter. Then stir in the apples and onions followed by the brown sugar, cloves, chilli powder, turmeric, ginger and vinegar, and season with salt and pepper. Mix well. Cover the saucepan, increase the heat and bring to the boil. Reduce the heat and leave to simmer over a medium heat for 20 minutes, stirring every 5 minutes.

Remove the lid, reduce the heat and leave to cook for a further 30 minutes until the apples have broken down and the chutney has turned a rich, golden brown. Use the back of a wooden spoon to crush the apples. Remove the pan from the heat and leave to cool; the chutney will thicken more as it cools.

Once the chutney has cooled, spoon it into 12 sterilised jars, seal and label.

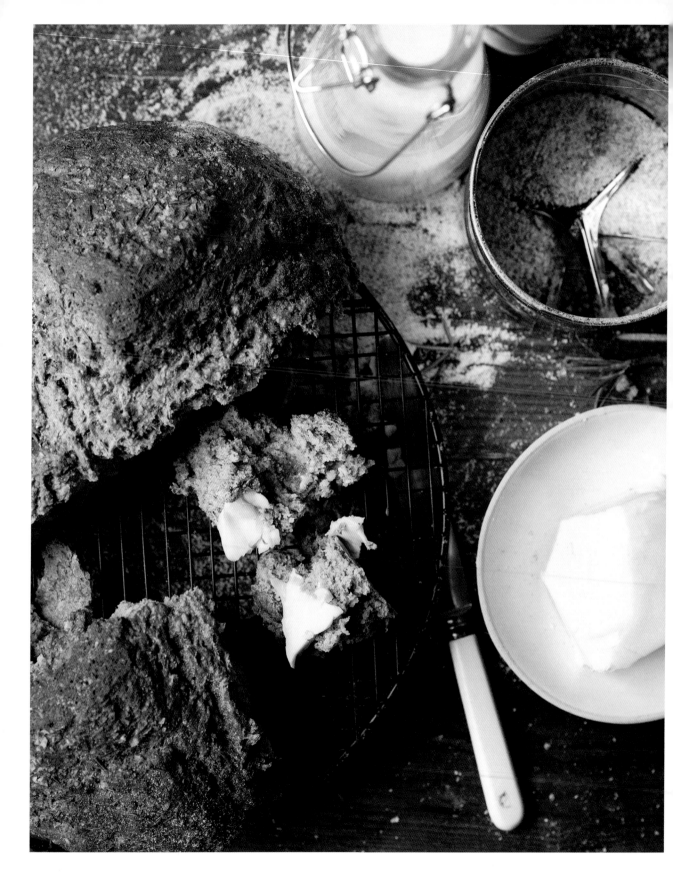

Rosemary Clodagh Bread

MAKES 1 LOAF

No matter what supper I am cooking, I always serve this bread in the centre of the table and I ask my guests to break the bread with me. This is a big tradition in my home, for me it symbolises the beginning of the supper, a shared and peaceful offering. It is a very simple bread to make as there is no kneading or resting involved. It's a take on the traditional Irish soda bread – it's wholesome and crumbly but doesn't leave you feeling bloated like some yeast breads can. It takes 20 minutes to prepare and then it's straight in the oven.

200g white flour, plus extra for dusting

2 teaspoons bicarbonate of soda

350g wholemeal flour

2 tablespoons finely chopped rosemary

1 teaspoon sea salt

250ml natural yogurt

350ml milk

milk and yogurt mix, for brushing

Preheat your oven to 220°C/gas mark 7.

Sift the white flour and bicarbonate of soda into a large mixing bowl and stir in the wholemeal flour, half the rosemary and the sea salt. Using clean hands, mix the dry ingredients together and make a well in the centre of the bowl.

Whisk together the yogurt and milk and slowly pour into the well of the dry ingredients. Use your free hand to mix the dough lightly, spreading your fingers far apart. Make sure that there are no dry patches and that the dough is completely wet.

Pat your hands with flour and shape the dough into one round. Place on a floured baking tray. Flour a large knife and cut the shape of a cross into the top of the dough about two-thirds of the way through.

Brush the dough with the milk and yogurt mixture using a pastry brush, this will give a lovely golden colour to the bread once baked, and sprinkle the remaining chopped rosemary on top.

Bake for 25 minutes, then reduce the heat to 180°C/gas mark 4 and bake for a further 25 minutes. To test whether the loaf is cooked, tap the bottom with your knuckles; it should sound hollow. Leave to cool on a cooling rack.

Index

Acknowledgements

I want to start by thanking Kyle Cathie, one of the most dedicated publishers in this business who is now retired. She made sure to get this book commissioned before she left, always believing in me and the ideas that I have. Thank you Kyle from the bottom of my heart. You are missed...

Dora Kazmierak, the photographer for this book. Dora has been a friend of mine for many years and has put endless hours into helping me create this very special book. Dora, you are so talented and I love watching you grow and grow. I am so excited that this is your first book, hooray!

Lizzie Harris, who cooked all the delicious dishes in the book. Lizzie, I absolutely adore you! You are the most talented chef and kindest person. Thank you for putting so much care into making each recipe look so good!

Vicky Orchard, the editor. Thank you Vicky for keeping me on track and arranging so much to make this a joy to work on.

Lucy Gowans, the designer. Thank you for making the pages look so beautiful and perfectly aligned! Wei Tang, the props stylist. Thank you for gathering so many beautiful props for me to play with!

Harry Herbert, my amazing boyfriend. Thank you for the hours you have spent reading over this book and finding all my little mistakes, for eating all my recipes and for being a constant positive voice. I love you with all my heart.

To all my dear friends – Hannah Pawlby, Anoushka Healy, Thea Rogers, Fiona Leahy, Nikki Tibbles, Sally Greene, my sister Mairead McKenna, plus many more. Thank you all so much for your support from the very beginning when I first started to try to get this book published. For giving me so much advice and for eating all my dishes with enthusiasm! You are all such a massive part of this book. I am very lucky to have you all...

And to you, for buying this book, cooking the recipes and sharing my love for suppers at home.

Love, Clo xxx